For Victor's eightieth birthday his right-hand man prepares a special celebration — a country feast in the heart of the city, twenty-seven storeys up. But Victor is making preparations of his own, to leave his mark upon the city, as indelible and disruptive as the mark his city left him.
The scene is set for

Arcadia...

the dream of those who live in cities

JIM CRACE *Arcadia*

'One thinks of Calvino and Coetzee for comparisons but in fact Crace is an original' RUSSELL BANKS

'The novelist for the Nineties' MALCOLM BRADBURY

19 MARCH 1992 • £14.99 • ISBN 0224 026925 • JONATHAN CAPE

ROYAL
COURT
THEATRE

JULIET STEVENSON

BILL PATERSON   MICHAEL BYRNE

DEATH AND THE MAIDEN

BY ARIEL DORFMAN

'A TERRIFYING MORAL THRILLER'
SUNDAY TIMES

'ONE OF THE YEAR'S ESSENTIAL PLAYS'
DAILY MAIL

'IT SHOULD NOT BE MISSED'
FINANCIAL TIMES

DIRECTED BY
LINDSAY POSNER

DESIGNED BY
IAN MacNEIL

LIGHTING BY
KEVIN SLEEP

THE
DUKE OF YORK'S THEATRE
SOLE PROPRIETOR: DUKE OF YORK'S THEATRE LTD   ST MARTIN'S LANE WC2

BOX OFFICE 071 836 5122 cc 071 836 9837

GRANTA

THE BODY

39

Editor: Bill Buford
Deputy Editor: Tim Adams
Managing Editor: Ursula Doyle
Editorial Assistant: Robert McSweeney
Contributing Editor: Rose Kernochan

Managing Director: Derek Johns
Financial Controller: Geoffrey Gordon
Circulation Manager: Sally Lewis

Picture Editor: Alice Rose George
Executive Editor: Pete de Bolla
US Associate Publisher: Anne Kinard, Granta, 250 West 57th Street, Suite 1316, New York, NY 10107.

Editorial and Subscription Correspondence: Granta, 2–3 Hanover Yard, Noel Road, Islington, London N1 8BE. Telephone: (071) 704 9776. Fax: (071) 704 0474. Subscriptions: (071) 704 0470.
A one-year subscription (four issues) is £19.95 in Britain, £27.95 for the rest of Europe, and £34.95 for the rest of the world.
All manuscripts are welcome but must be accompanied by a stamped, self-addressed envelope or they cannot be returned.

Granta is printed in the United States of America. The paper used in this publication meets the minimum requirements of American National Standard for Information Sciences—Permanence of Paper for Printed Library Materials, ANSI Z39.48-1984 ∞

Cover by Senate. Photo: Antonin Kratochvil

Granta 39, Spring 1992
ISBN 0-14-014050-6

Graham Swift's WATERLAND was *the*
classic British novel of the 1980s.
Now comes his classic British novel
for the 1990s...

GRAHAM SWIFT
Ever After

'It begins in mystery and ends in revelation;
what it reveals may be the most beautiful love
story in contemporary literature'
MICHAEL HERR

Waterland – **NEW PICADOR HARDBACK EDITION**

OUTSTANDING INTERNATIONAL WRITING

PICADOR

THE GRANTA BOOK OF THE AMERICAN SHORT STORY

720 PAGES OF THE BEST SHORT FICTION PUBLISHED IN AMERICA SINCE 1946 INCLUDING THE WORK OF

RAYMOND CARVER, JAYNE ANNE PHILLIPS, JOHN CHEEVER

JOY WILLIAMS, T C BOYLE, JOHN UPDIKE, LORRIE MOORE

GRACE PALEY, BARRY HANNAH AND DAVID LEAVITT

Edited by
RICHARD
FORD

The End of Science...?

Bryan Appleyard's

devastating analysis of the assault
of science and the way it has
shaped our lives.

Understanding The Present

SCIENCE AND THE SOUL OF MODERN MAN

'Required reading for anyone who wants
fully to understand the meaning of the
late 20th century'
PETER ACKROYD

'The account sings...Appleyard is
excellent at spelling out in layman's
language the intricacies of
Quantum Theory'
ROY PORTER

A PICADOR HARDBACK AVAILABLE FROM 8 MAY

OUTSTANDING INTERNATIONAL WRITING

FROM ONE OF AMERICA'S MOST DAZZLING
NEW WRITERS, THE CELEBRATED AUTHOR OF
THE MYSTERIES OF PITTSBURGH

MICHAEL CHABON

A Model World

& OTHER STORIES

'Admirable . . . stories with a welcome wryness'
Adam Mars-Jones in The Independent on Sunday Books of the Year

'With this volume Chabon goes beyond the promise
of his last book. Indeed he establishes himself as one
of his generation's most eloquent new voices'
The New York Times

PUBLISHES 2ND APRIL

£5.99

CONTENTS

TIMOTHY MO

THE REDUNDANCY OF COURAGE

SHORTLISTED FOR THE 1991 BOOKER PRIZE

TOLD IN THE VOICE OF A YOUNG CHINESE HOTEL-OWNER
ADOLPH NG, TIMOTHY MO'S FIRST NOVEL IS AN
ENTHRALLING EXPLORATION OF COURAGE AND BETRAYAL

"Mo's incisive portrayal of the conflict between
human needs and political expediency shudders
with contemporary resonance"

THE TIMES

£6.99

JOHN D. BARROW

THEORIES OF EVERYTHING

THE HOLY GRAIL OF MODERN SCIENTISTS IS THE
"THEORY OF EVERYTHING", WHICH WILL CONTAIN ALL THAT
CAN BE KNOWN ABOUT THE UNIVERSE. IN THIS ELEGANT AND
EXCITING BOOK, JOHN BARROW CHALLENGES THE QUEST FOR
ULTIMATE EXPLANATION

"Bridges the gap between the research frontiers of
theoretical physics and the aspirations of the man
on the Clapham omnibus to understand what is going on"

TIMES LITERARY SUPPLEMENT

£6.99

VINTAGE PAPERBACKS

REDMOND O'HANLON
THE CONGO DINOSAUR

The Congo Dinosaur

T he boy lay stretched out on a low wooden platform under an orange tree. His father sat on a stool beside him, bending forward, chanting at the top of his voice, over and over again, 'I've lost my child. My poor son. My son is dead.' Twenty or so women, sitting on mats behind him, rocked back and forth, wailing in chorus.

I squatted nearby on the roots of a mango tree. I was with the principal companion of my journey through the forests of the northern Congo, Doctor Marcellin Agnagna, the Cuban-educated head of the Ministry for the Conservation of Fauna and Flora, and two of his young nephews: Nzé, our cook, whose left eye, in moments of relaxation, pointed to the sky while his right one was focused on the ground, and Manou, too weakened by attacks of malaria to be much more than my quiet informant. Djéké was by far the largest, best ordered, most advanced village I had seen in three months of travel: you could walk for almost two kilometres through its plantations of manioc and bananas, cacao and plantains; it even had a little shop. And having bought coffee and sugar for the mourners, a goat for the father and a winding-sheet for the corpse, I felt I had a right to ask a question.

'What happened?'

Doctor Marcellin put a finger to his lips and shook his head at me.

Mourners continued to arrive. I spotted Léonard Bongou-Lami, Commandant of the People's Militia of Djéké (and my temporary translator from Bomitaba into French).

'This is the right way to do things,' I said lamely. 'It's wonderful to share your grief with everyone. We don't deal with death like this in England.'

The Commandant turned on me. 'But the father,' he said, pausing to spit, 'killed his own children. He did it himself.'

'What do you mean?'

'He killed his wife, *and then all five children*. He's a sorcerer. We're all frightened of him.'

Without looking back, the Commandant walked off and joined another crowd of onlookers.

Opposite: Lac Télé in the northern Congo.

13

Around dusk, a group of men pushed past, bearing an eight-foot-high drum. They were followed by a gaggle of boys carrying chopped wood who made small fires round the centre of the enclosure. Bats as big as blackbirds appeared, their wings creaking as they laboured over us. The fire burst into life and the men picked up the drum and held it with its top towards the flames to warm its skin. Night fell with equatorial abruptness.

Doctor Marcellin, whom I'd sought out in Brazzaville and persuaded to come with me because he was the one man who swore he'd seen the Congo dinosaur, Mokele-mbembe—three hundred yards out in Lac Télé, with a hippo-sized body and a long neck, a brown face and black back (on which the sun glinted)—took the pipe I'd given him out of his trouser pocket, filled it from our last remaining tin of tobacco, lit up and inhaled deeply. His mistress of two nights, young, eager and beautiful, came and sat between us. She gazed at him in the firelight.

An old man appeared, put his head back, held out his arms and shouted into the darkness towards the forest.

'Who's he calling?' Marcellin asked the girl to translate.

'He says that his grandson Kotéla loved to dance,' she whispered, 'so we must show how much we miss him by dancing. And he calls to the ghosts in the forest: "If god took young Kotéla, then god took him; but if young Kotéla died because of sorcery, then, spirits, search out the sorcerer and kill him now."'

Men formed one half of a circle, women the other. The drum, judged to be ready, was set up in the centre and a platform brought for the drummer. He produced a massive sound; another man beat the trunk of the drum with two short sticks, and the dance began. The two nephews, Nzé and Manou, drifted back to our guest-hut, and Marcellin, his mistress and I joined the dance: five steps forward, a half turn to the left, a half turn to the right, five steps back and on round the circle. After two or three hours, during which we danced the *mozambique*, the *mobenga* and the *ekogo*, Marcellin said goodbye to the girl and then we, too, made our way back to where we were staying.

Children ran past us, carrying lemons to their parents at the dance, up late with the licence of the fiesta, wide-eyed and quick with excitement. I felt, walking under this moon and these unfamiliar stars, beneath the tiny orange glow of the Russian observation satellite hanging stationary in space above the Marxist People's Republic of the Congo, that Djéké itself was a village in an idyll, a place where nothing bad could happen.

In the guest-hut Doctor Marcellin lit a candle, and I took out the gourd of palm wine I had bought that afternoon. Nzé and Manou were waiting for us.

'Redmon,' said Nzé, pleased with himself, skew-eyed and sweaty in the Cuban army fatigues and peaked cloth cap of the People's Militia of Dongou, 'I need 500 CFAs.'

'Not yet, you don't,' said Doctor Marcellin. 'You'll make our supper first.'

I got the 500 francs (the equivalent of one pound) from my bergen pack. A pound a night was the going rate.

'But Nzé,' I said, 'I've only just cured the gonorrhoea you got in Enyellé. That was the last twelve Amoxil.'

'Your western medicine didn't help at all,' said Nzé, picking up the pot of our left-over monkey stew and taking it outside to place on the fire. 'I was discharging for three days afterwards.' He turned round for greater emphasis, flicking his free hand down his crotch to mime a stream of falling pus. 'And then when I drank the bottle of bark-water my brother gave me, it went at once. He made it in the way our grandfather taught him. That's what did it. That's why I'm cured.' He squatted down, arranging the fire. 'My grandfather was the greatest sorcerer in Dongou, Redmon. Even more powerful than the Chief of Dongou. The Chief of Dongou visited my grandfather once, in the spirit way, but my grandfather won the battle and took away the Chief of Dongou's clothes—and in the morning he made the Chief of Dongou walk in his sleep from one end of Dongou to the other and back again, in the nude, with his dick standing up. *That* taught him a lesson.'

'It's not as funny as you think,' said Manou. 'Take that poor father. They say he killed his son, but that's not so. He did only one thing wrong. Long ago, he arrived at his uncle's wedding without a present of drink or money. His uncle was a sorcerer, so he said: "Right, when you get married and have children of your

15

own, I'll kill them all. I'll wait until they're fourteen or fifteen years old, each one, and then, when you love them more than anything on earth, they'll die slowly in front of you."'

'That's not what I heard,' said Doctor Marcellin. 'I heard that the father *did* kill his own children, but he didn't mean to do it. He visited a *féticheur* to get a fetish for his own protection. That was all right. But then he asked for a fetish that would make him a great fisherman. And that was his mistake. "Put so-and-so in a bottle," said the *féticheur*, "something that you really value, and then throw it in the river." And that's what he did. But then his child died so he went to a second *féticheur*, who said "Yes, well what did you expect? When you cut those locks of hair from all your children's heads and put them in that bottle and threw it in the river you threw away their futures. It's simple. All you have to do is get your bottle back at once, or all your children will die." But it wasn't simple. The river here is a blackwater river, and you can't see into it, and he spent three months trailing the mud with his nets and found nothing. And now his last child is dead.'

'So what do you think it is really?' I said. 'Hereditary leukaemia? Haemophilia? Something like that?'

'You and your white man's questions,' said Doctor Marcellin. 'That's not what really *matters*.'

Nzé doled out the monkey stew and a piece of *fufu* (manioc stodge) into our mess tins.

'So, Marcellin, why don't you want to go to Boha and Lac Télé? Is that a matter of sorcery too?'

'You don't understand, Redmond. You don't understand the risk I'm taking. They'll murder me. Boha is a village unlike anywhere else. They hunt the gorilla and the chimpanzee, in preference to all other meat. They use special spears that are twelve feet long. The young men provoke the male gorilla, until he charges on to their points.' He jumped to his feet, yelled and impaled me in the chest with an imaginary spear—with excessive enthusiasm, I thought, for the head of conservation. Calming himself, he sat down again. 'There are all kinds of problems. The young men loyal to the traditional chief kill the men loyal to the Party. Almost all the men of Boha have been put in prison at

Epéna and locked up for five days—the punishment for a murder that is domestic or a matter of sorcery. The Political Commissar of the People's District of Epéna put a policeman at Boha once, but he ran away. We also will run away.'

'Why?'

'Because they think I put their *Chief* in prison. And that's a terrible insult to them. They've taken a blood-oath to kill me if I ever set foot in Boha again. I have one friend there—the mother of a young man who works for me in the department in Brazzaville. She sent a warning to my mother in Impfondo.'

'How come you put the Chief in prison?'

'I didn't. After my last expedition, the all-Congolese expedition, when we saw the dinosaur, I wrote in my report that the Chief made us pay 75,000 CFAs to enter his forests. I had to, Redmond; I had to account for the money I spent to our minister in Brazzaville. And when the Political Commissar of the People's District of Epéna saw the report he said that the Chief of Boha must be taught that he does not run an independent state. So he called in the army and they went downriver with big outboards and forty soldiers and captured the Chief at dawn when he was still asleep with his wives and they took him back to Epéna and locked him in the People's Prison for three whole days.'

'But it's ridiculous,' I said, suddenly inspired. 'You're the head of conservation for all of the People's Republic of the Congo. You're a very important chief in your own right. You can't pretend to be in charge and then have areas you're too frightened to visit. We've got to see your dinosaur. We'll leave in the morning.'

'I've had enough,' said Marcellin, jumping to his feet. He was rigid with anger; for a moment I thought he was going to hit me. 'I'm leaving,' he said. 'I'm going to see my girl.'

Nzé drew the door aside, but Marcellin, even in his rage, remembered to return to his pack, reach into its side-pocket, and pull out the bottle of aftershave I'd given him in Brazzaville. He sprayed himself inside the front of his shirt, replaced the bottle, and, in a cloud of scent, disappeared into the night.

Nzé peered round the door. Satisfied that Marcellin had really gone, he lunged at the pack, snatched the magic bottle, sprayed himself so hard he sneezed, tucked it back, mimed a few practice thrusts up against the wall, announced that 'He's not the only one who has a woman!' and followed Doctor Marcellin into the darkness.

Manou sat with his head in his hands, his palm wine untouched.

'What's the matter?' I said. 'You don't believe it, do you? You don't think there's any danger?'

'Of course it's dangerous,' said Manou, unusually quiet, even for him. 'They'll kill you, too.'

'Why me? It's nothing to do with me.'

'It's everything to do with you,' said Manou. 'It's a white man's problem. It's white people like you who cause all the trouble.'

'I don't understand.'

'It's simple. Marcellin wants white people to come here to see Lac Télé. He says his minister will set up a national park and make him rich. He told the men of Boha that if they didn't like it he'd call in the army and have the village moved somewhere else. But the men of Boha can't move. The lake is three days' walk away in the forest, it's true, but that is where the spirits of their ancestors live. If the villagers are moved any further, everyone will die. The ancestors will no longer protect them.'

Manou stopped and said nothing. Seeing that he was starting to fall asleep, I decided that it was probably the right time to go to bed myself. I blew out the candle, unzipped my tent, climbed through the opening, strapped on my head-torch, caught a couple of mosquitoes which had followed me in, put fresh Savlon and plasters on the tsetse-fly bites that had ulcerated on my swollen legs and ankles, and, from a plastic bag in the document wallet in the lid of my pack, drew out a sheaf of photocopies I had made in Oxford. They were chapters from Roy Mackal's *A Living Dinosaur? In Search of Mokele-Mbembe* (1987). Mackal himself had never reached Lac Télé, but Doctor Marcellin Agnagna, with an all-Congolese expedition, later made another attempt. And that one had been successful.

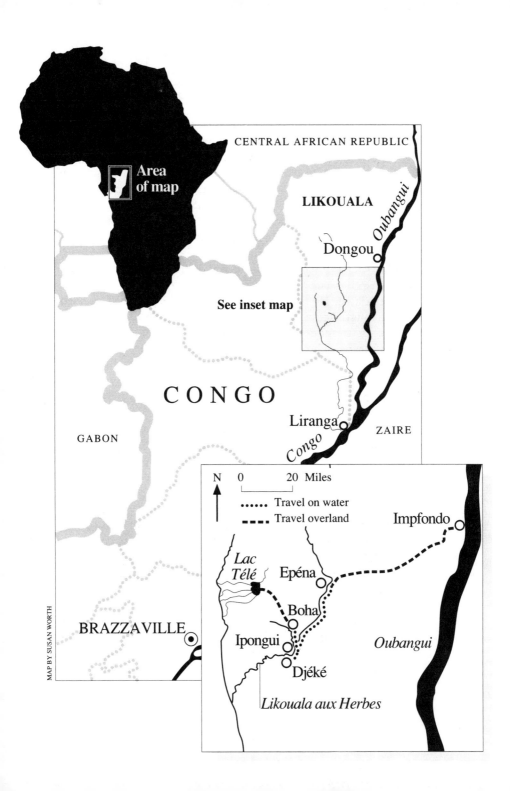

CENTRAL AFRICAN REPUBLIC

LIKOUALA

Oubangui

Dongou

See inset map

CONGO

Liranga

GABON

ZAIRE

Congo

Area
of map

BRAZZAVILLE

N   0   20 Miles

······· Travel on water
------- Travel overland

Lac
Télé

Epéna

Impfondo

Boha

Ipongui

Djéké

Oubangui

Likouala aux Herbes

MAP BY SUSAN WORTH

2

At first light, our tethered cockerel crowed five feet from my head, his challenge at once answered by the local champion with a burst of outrage from the other side of the door. I put on my boots and binoculars, unzipped the tent, stole a few spoonfuls of last night's (already left-over) male-monkey stew (still tasting of unwashed crotch), clattered back to the door, eased the cockerel aside with my foot and took a deep breath of the morning mist. Some mad woman laughed at me.

Confused, I traced the hysterical chuckle to the top of a straggly tree. It was a kingfisher. A small blaze of iridescent azure in the grey dawn. He must be the Congo blue-breasted, I decided, the freak kingfisher who never fishes, lives in the forest, makes his home in termite nests in high trees and eats only frogs, scorpions, crabs, whip-scorpions, cockroaches, beetles, mantises, toads, spiders and millipedes. Deciding, in his turn, that I was too big to be interesting, he gave a final descending laugh of disappointment, dropped sharply out of the tree and flew off fast and low.

Crouching behind a bush by the manioc plantation, I looked up from a spasm of diarrhoea in time to spot another misfit curving overhead towards the river, the vulturine fish eagle, the only (mainly) vegetarian bird of prey in the world (it has a passion for palm-nuts). And walking back, I disrupted the sex-life of the pin-tailed whidah, a sparrow-sized bird with a white stomach, a blue back and bright red beak—and a tail of two long black plumes, which he held beneath him while jerking rapidly to and fro, fluttering his wings, a little bundle of feathers in the last stages of ejaculatory passion. Three dull brown females pecked about on the ground beneath him, unimpressed by the frantic adulation a yard above their heads.

Back in the hut, Manou was listlessly packing the cooking-pot and mess tins into an old manioc sack.

Our paddlers arrived along with my translator, the Commandant, and I handed out paracetamol, plasters and fifteen glossy white quinine pills to everyone. Together we carried our baggage down to the creek that led on to the main stream of the Likouala-aux-Herbes river.

The Commandant stowed our packs in the middle of his dug-out; Manou gently placed the wicker cage containing our cock and two hens in the bow; and we settled down on the short scuffed grass of the bank to wait for Nzé and Doctor Marcellin. Downstream, a young mother was sitting on the upturned hull of a half-submerged dug-out, its grey wood worn smooth from scrubbing and pounding clothes. She wore an indigo cotton dress wrapped round tight just above her nipples and dipping low across her muscled back, and her hair twirled out in two spikes like radio antennae. Washed pots and pans lay stacked on one side, clothes on the other, and between her knees she gripped her toddler son. She cuddled him while scooping up a saucepanful of water and dumping it on his head. He howled as if his world had disappeared, screamed as the soap ran into his eyes, gurgled for air in the final rinse and then, the moment it was over, opened his eyes, beamed at us and clapped his hands. We all clapped back and she kissed him, but, overcome with such success, he dived for cover, sinking his head between her breasts.

The mother smiled, said something to the Commandant and launched her son for a swim in the shallows. Much laughter and bantering in Bomitaba took place.

'She thinks you don't know how to dance,' said the Commandant. 'She says you just shake yourself all over, like a dog fresh out of water. You must learn to use your legs, Redmon, like a man of good manners. You must not tread on people with those big boots of yours.'

'It's true,' said Manou drowsily, lying on his back and sucking on a grass stem, 'and you're not supposed to wave your arms around.'

There was a shout from the top of the path. It was Nzé. 'Five times!' he yelled. 'Five times for 500 CFAs! 100 CFAs a time! And just look what she gave me!'

He raised his arms in triumph, and in each hand he held a pineapple.

Doctor Marcellin appeared at the top of the bank and the laughter ceased. He was not his usual self. He came down the

21

path, barking questions like a Nazi. Why had we left the hut so early? Where was his breakfast? And why, he wanted to know, stepping into the dug-out, was his pack at the bottom of the pile? Why were there no duck-boards? What if his shirts got wet? Who had done this to him?

Marcellin, I thought, does not want to leave his young girl. But then it gradually dawned on me, as I watched him yank his pack to the top of the pile, scrabble at a pocket, pull out his Walkman, ferociously snap in a Bob Marley tape, cover his ears with the headphones, sink back against the baggage and close his eyes: Marcellin was afraid. He really did think there would be trouble at Boha.

The north Congo flood-plain of the Likouala-aux-Herbes is a narrow savannah; the high forest began again a mile or so to either side of us. At first we were all as silent as Marcellin, but then the three boys began their paddling songs, the rhythm in time with the long blades cutting down and thrusting back in the water.

'We burn the grass during the dry season,' said the Commandant, 'not to hunt the animals or make plantations for manioc, but to keep the paths open to the forest.' He let his paddle rest against the gunwale a moment and gestured out across the high grass, the lone trees beside the river, the patches of water-lilies. 'I like it here,' he said. 'When I was in Brazzaville, I missed all this.'

'Why were you in Brazzaville?'

'I wanted to be rich. I found work on a building site. But poor men like me can't get rich in the city. Everything costs money. You even have to pay to live in a house! So then I realized that it was in my own village that I was rich. Here you make your home from the earth, you can grow manioc wherever you choose, you can make a boat and nets and fish in the river—me, I'm happy here.'

'And now you're the Commandant of the People's Militia.'

'Oh *that*,' he said, laughing. 'In Djéké that's just a joke.

Opposite: Nzé, in the dug-out, with pineapples.

That's just an excuse to get a pair of trousers from the government. Gilbert Badiledi is the *Commandant d'Honneur* but I'm the *Commandant Actif,* so I can tell the *Chargé* and the *Adjudant de Compagnie* what to do, and I can see the Hereditary Chief and the President of the People's Village Committee whenever I feel like it, and then we have lots of militiamen who are almost as useless as Nzé—and I'm allowed to *shout* at them.'

'You should come to Dongou and say that,' said Nzé, from behind the baggage. 'We'd soon sort you out. We've got proper uniforms and proper houses and a bar,' he said, turning over and going back to sleep.

'In Boha,' said the Commandant, 'it is not a joke. In Boha they killed the officers. There are no militiamen in Boha.'

'Commandant,' said Marcellin, who must have been listening, 'in Boha you and your three nephews will stay with us for the first night.'

'No, Marcellin Agnagna, not for all the money you've got in your pack. Not for all the young girls you care to give me. I'm a sensible man. And besides, I have a baby son. Soon he will need a father.'

'I am the official representative of the government here,' said Marcellin, suddenly sitting up, 'and I order you to stay for one night.'

'You can order all you like,' said the Commandant. 'One hour will be enough for me. And even then you must watch your back. They've been taking oaths in Boha.'

We passed a long beach of white sand, almost too bright to look at in the sunlight—perhaps part of the friable white sandstone that formed beneath the great lake which filled the Congo basin some 225 million years ago, when you could see dinosaurs every day of the week. And upriver we came to a low overhang of dark grey soil and a stretch of scrubby trees.

Small blue-green birds, blue-cheeked bee-eaters, were perched on the branches, fussing over their long tail feathers. They flew out fast like swallows, low across the water, and then up and above our heads towards the rough grass of the savannah, their undersides glowing orange in the reflected light.

The Commandant nodded towards a tall tree with thin

branches and small leaves which hung out over the water.

'That's a fishing tree,' he said. 'When the fruits are ripe they turn yellow and drop into the river and the fish gather: there's one little fruit for each fish. That's the time to bring your nets.'

We passed a small village hidden behind its oil-palms on a piece of high ground, which the Commandant said was called Ipongui. Whenever there was the slightest hint of another human being in the landscape—the splash of a paddle up a creek, smoke from the roof of one of the lone huts on the bank—the Commandant shouted a greeting in Bomitaba, and news was exchanged for a good hundred yards or more at an ever-increasing volume.

In a stretch of comparative quiet, by a shore of white sand, I recognized a bird wading carefully in the shallows. It was brown all over, rook-size, but its head was remarkable: a big, broad bill balanced by a triangular crest at the back gave its head the shape of an anvil—a hammerkop. It walked slowly, concentrating on the water surface as it shuffled its feet, stirring up the sand to flush out small fish, molluscs and beetles, letting us come very close before it rose jerkily into the air on surprisingly broad wings, its head stretched out, light and silent as an owl. The hammerkop was impossible to classify. It was thought to be related to the herons, or possibly the flamingos, or even the shoebill; but recent egg-white protein analysis put it closest to the storks, while the parasites on its skin related it to the plovers, snipes and sandpipers. And its behaviour was all its own: the bird was known to throw some spectacularly open-minded parties. Eight to ten hammerkops would be invited, some unattached, some married, some divorced. They would turn up near the nest, everyone would pair off and they then ran in circles side by side until an orgy of (technically speaking) false mounting took place. No actual rubbing together of his everting and her receiving opposable vent was allowed in public, but you couldn't complain. The soliciting bird crouched down, the other mounted and balanced on top with open wings; and then, both of them shivering with the erotic charge of it all, they would press their tails together, the whole party accompanied by loud duets known as *yip-purring*. Males mounted females, females mounted males, males mounted males, and only lesbians were disadvantaged.

Just as I was thinking about all this sex, and wondering why, as far as I could remember, so few birds actually had a penis (only the ostrich, the rhea, the emu, the cassowary, the tinamou, the duck and the screamer), the Commandant swung the bow of the dug-out into a small tributary, and I realized that we had arrived at Boha.

3

'Quick!' said Marcellin, as we put in to a landing-stage, grabbing the gun from the bottom of the dug-out and bounding past me, 'get up into the village and in among some women and children. And don't get separated.' His white basketball boots sprayed pebbles off the sandstone path. 'Nzé! Manou!' he shouted over his shoulder. 'Stay right by me! Commandant! You and the paddlers. You follow with the packs. You must stay for one hour. Just one hour. Redmond will pay you in one hour.'

Nzé, Manou and I ran hard and caught up with Marcellin at the top of the path. He had his arm round an old man, outside the open lean-to of a cooking-hut. 'Bobé!' he shouted, not letting go, 'Bobé, my old friend!'

Bobé, bemused but happy, smiled, showing his gums. Barefoot, he wore torn, dirty white cotton trousers rolled up his shins and a red-and-white-striped pyjama top opened to his bony chest and wizened stomach.

A group of children, attracted by the noise, appeared in the space between the huts.

'*Mondelé!*' they shouted, '*Mondelé! Mondelé!*' (White man! White man!).

The children pressed around us, and the boldest, a boy of five or six, held up a grasshopper for my inspection. He was pinching it by its back legs, between his index finger and thumb, and as I bent down to admire it—noting the light green of its rear end, the yellow on its back beneath a slight all-over froth, the white spots on its red, black and yellow head—he jammed it up into my nostril. I leaped backwards, my sinuses full of acrid musk like the pong of a dead stoat. Warning colours, I thought ruefully, in between sneezes; this must be one of those forest grasshoppers that makes such a stink of itself that no sensible predator goes near it. The children jumped up and down with delight, the boy turned away with one of those half-private smiles that only personal triumph produces—and suddenly they all scattered away between the huts.

Four broad-shouldered young men were swaggering towards us down the right-hand path. I walked up to shake their hands but they brushed past me and surrounded Marcellin. Nzé, who had seized the gun, pointed the barrel at their feet. He patted the stock. Marcellin did not look reassured.

'You will come with us,' said the leader in French. 'We will talk at the table of the Vice-President of the People's Village Committee.'

In the silence, while Marcellin apparently considered the offer, I found myself staring at their T-shirts. The leader, heavy-faced, wore a plea from the World Wildlife Fund across his massive chest, '*Ne tuez pas les gorilles et les chimpanzes*'; a string round his cotton trousers held a dagger at his side, about fifteen inches long. One of his lieutenants sported a blue vest with 'Woods Hole Oceanographic Institution' emblazoned on the front; another had 'Harley-Davidson' on a green background; and the third displayed a cartoon of a man eating popcorn, ogling a big-breasted woman flopped beside a swimming-pool with her husband approaching stage left. The legend read, 'IT'S A NICE AFTERNOON FOR BILL, BUT BE CAREFUL, FIGHT MAYBE COME.'

Disappointed that Boha was obviously so visited, I started matching up the intruders to their T-shirts: the first three would have been left here by the American Philip Lobel of Woods Hole who, according to Marcellin, claimed to have discovered forty-five new species of fish in Lac Télé; and the last came perhaps from the Japanese dinosaur-hunting expedition of 1988. The Commandant and his nephews appeared, laden with baggage. Marcellin gave a nod, and we followed Doubla into the village.

27

The village was much smaller than Djéké, with winding paths leading away from one short broad street. There were fewer gardens and only the occasional hut of clay bricks among the mud and thatch.

I paused to watch a middle-aged man, his head shaved, working at his kiln. He was building a new house in his enclosure and, sweating, barefoot, in only a pair of ragged shorts, was feeding logs into a clay block furnace that had been plastered with mud to retain the heat. He looked round and gave me a friendly flash of gappy white teeth. Simultaneously I felt a little hand creep into mine.

The bold boy, now without his grasshopper, beamed up at me. He looked new, ready for life, as yet untouched by disease of any kind, and he talked fast in Bomitaba about something so special and pressing that my inability to reply seemed not to matter. Marcellin and the others had disappeared, so I allowed my new guide to pull me along a path branching off to the right. His gang, now swollen to a band of twenty or so, followed at a respectful distance, still chanting *'Mondelé! Mondelé!'* and pointing at me as proof.

A little further on, we came to the object of our quest. The boy tugged at my hand, and we all processed into a small enclosure and up to the entrance of a hut where, suspended beneath the shelter of the overhanging thatch, a green fruit-pigeon sat bedraggled in a cage.

The boy talked to it, and the pigeon cocked its head and listened. One of the children eased a piece of papaya through the bars. The pigeon was green all over except for a purple patch on its shoulder, the black on its wings and a blue tail. Quiet, mating for life, it is so sensitive that it is reputed to die of shock at the sound of a gun. I was just beginning to feel sorry for it when the boy yanked at my hand again and we were off round the corner and down a little incline to another hut. Five young children and two women sat on a raffia mat. They smiled. Behind them stood Marcellin, Nzé, Manou, the Commandant and his paddlers.

'Where the hell have you been?' said Marcellin.

The boy let go of my hand.

Marcellin moved forward and stood over me. 'I thought I

told you not to get separated,' he hissed into my ear. 'Just do what I say, will you? You do not understand. *You are now out of your depth.*'

And you are out of your mind, I thought crossly, until a piece of genuine fear moved in my stomach like the first warning of oncoming dysentery. Four young men in torn camouflage fatigues stood motionless under a safou tree twenty paces away. They held outrageously long spears, the beaten-iron blades tilted at the ground, the shafts stretching way up and back over their shoulders.

'Where did they get those uniforms?'

'From the Japanese,' said Marcellin without looking round, 'on my last expedition. But please, Redmond, *no more questions.*'

A thin, nervous, middle-aged man stepped out of the hut.

'Are you ready?' he said.

'Yes, *Monsieur le Vice-President,*' said Marcellin. 'Now we can talk.'

Nzé, looking uncharacteristically serious, stood guard by the door with the gun. The Commandant and the paddlers sat down in the shade and Marcellin, Manou and I filed into the hut behind the Vice-President.

I took the chair by the door, the sunlight bright and hard on the baked ground outside. On the wall was a picture from a magazine, a portrait of the President of the People's Republic of the Congo, Colonel Denis Sassou-Nguesso, wearing a red parachute-regiment beret, dark glasses and fatigues, and leaning with both hands firmly on a balcony rail, a big pistol at his belt. I wondered if that was the same service revolver that was rumoured to have got him the job—by exploding the head of the previous incumbent all over the wall of the presidential dining-room. It was mysterious, people said with a touch of admiration; two men went in to breakfast and only one came out: somehow Captain Marien Ngouabi had got himself assassinated.

Marcellin sat beside me, and the men in the exotic T-shirts entered. Their leader, the giant wearing the plea for gorillas and chimpanzees, placed himself at the head of the table. The Vice-President sat at the other end. The giant demanded to see our papers. Marcellin unzipped his money and document pouch and produced our *Ordre de Service* from the *Secretariat General de L'Economie Forestière* and our *laissez-passer* from the *Ministère de la Recherche Scientifique et de L'Environnement.* They were passed from hand to hand around the table.

The giant turned his heavily lidded eyes on me. 'Your papers are in order,' he said, as if nothing else was.

'It's an honour to be here,' I said.

There was a scuffling noise in the passage and an old woman rushed into the room and seized Marcellin's arm. He followed her outside. When he returned moments later, he had a wild look in his eyes.

'It's all your fault,' he said to me in English. 'That's the mother of my friend in Brazzaville. They are going to murder me. She says we must run away. I should have brought my Kalashnikov. I didn't know we were coming here. You said we need not go to Boha. You lied to me. What about my little daughter? What about her? You should have brought me a pistol.'

'Marcellin,' said the Vice-President, returning the papers, 'the People's Village Committee demand to know one thing. Why did you put our Chief in prison? It is a great disgrace. Because you have come again to our village the Chief has taken his wives and hidden himself in the forest.'

'Why? What for?' said Marcellin, looking startled, his words rising to a high shout. 'What's he going to gain by that?'

Manou slid down the wall, slumped to a sitting position and put his head between his knees.

'Why did you put our Chief in prison?' said the giant in his preternaturally deep voice.

'It wasn't me,' said Marcellin, turning, bizarrely, to look at me, his eyes blankly searching my face.

'Marcellin Agnagna,' said the giant, 'when you reply to the questions of the People's Village Committee you will address yourself to the Vice-President of the People's Village Committee, and not to a white man.'

'It wasn't me,' repeated Marcellin. 'I am not a soldier. I am not a politician. I am under the power of the Political Commissar of the District of Epéna. I am a man of science.'

'You are a man of science,' said the giant, pointing a calloused finger at Marcellin's head, 'and that is why you came here with a bomb to kill the fish in our lake and to starve us to death.'

'That was not a bomb. That was a sonar. That was a machine to measure the depth of the water.'

'That's your story,' said the giant.

'There are men in the Party here who are jealous of me,' said Marcellin, his eyes flicking from one committee member to the next. 'They make a great noise and accuse me unjustly. The truth is we have different mentalities, you and I. I do not belong to your world. And that is why you are jealous of me.'

'You killed a gorilla,' said the giant. 'You tell us not to hunt the chimpanzees and the gorillas that belong to us and our ancestors, and then you kill a gorilla.'

'It was an old male. He was in a tree above our canoe. He was going to attack us.' Marcellin had become very excited. 'He was going to jump into our boat. So I fired.' Marcellin raised an imaginary gun.

'I don't believe you,' said the giant. 'We found dead turtles in the lake when you came with the small yellow men. We found dead antelope in the forest. The antelope and the turtles, they belong to us.'

'I have brought three expeditions here,' said Marcellin, raising his voice again. 'I have given many presents to the Chief. I have given many presents to the People's Village Committee. You should thank me. I bring fame to your village. They know your name in distant lands. And I ask you, can I help it—*is it my fault if the men with me transform themselves into animals in the night and go hunting where I cannot see them?* Eh? Am I responsible for that?'

'That is possible,' said the giant, seeming to contract in his chair, as if the argument had suddenly swung against him. 'But our Chief hides in the forest. He has nothing to say.'

'The white man has presents for him,' said Marcellin. 'He has a pipe from England, a knife, cloth for his wives and two pairs of shoes.'

There was a pause. 'You will stay where you are,' said the

31

giant at last. 'We will decide what to do with you.' He picked up his chair and carried it outside. The others followed.

'Get up, Manou,' said Marcellin, 'we share a mother. You must be a man.'

'I've got malaria,' said Manou, rising unsteadily to his feet. 'I'm shaking all over.'

'You shake because you are afraid,' said Marcellin, staring at the table-top in front of him. 'I promised our mother I'd make a man of you.' And then, without shifting his gaze, 'You've failed me, Redmond,' he said. 'I should have come with soldiers. These are not educated men. They kill gorillas and chimps and each other and tonight they will probably kill us too. Lac Télé is too precious to be left to such people. We should move these murderers to another village and bring in tourists and make money and protect the animals.'

A little boy peered round the door behind us, holding a yellow plastic football. He wiped his nose with one hand and lobbed the ball at me with the other. I patted it back.

'Don't talk to him,' said Marcellin. 'He's a spy.'

The giant leaned through the other door. 'We have decided,' he boomed. 'We will talk to the Chief. He will know what to do. The Vice-President will take you to the schoolmaster's house.'

We picked up our packs and followed the Vice-President down past the safou tree to the school playground, bounded on one side by a row of clay-brick schoolrooms roofed with thatch. The schoolmaster's hut was to our right.

'So, Marcellin,' I asked, 'where shall we pitch the tents?'

'No, Redmond, I'm not going to be axed through the canvas in the night. Not even for you. I know how you hate mosquitoes and chiggers, but tonight we sleep in a brick hut with only one door. Nzé and Manou will sleep across the door.'

'Remember Djéké, my friend,' said the Commandant, twisting his shoulders sideways to shed one of our bergens against the hut wall. 'Remember the place where you were happy, Redmon, because—you mark my words well—one way or another, the men of Boha will make you wish you'd never come to the Likouala.' He put his hand on my arm and looked anxiously into my eyes. 'You'll wish you'd never heard the name of our river, my friend.'

I paid him his 12,000 francs. He and the paddlers turned and left. They did not look back. The hut was very isolated, and ominously quiet.

Marcellin ordered Nzé to sleep by the door. 'And Redmond,' he said, 'is going to sleep with me.' He gave the bed a tremendous kick. There was a small rustling noise, like the movement of dry leaves. 'Bugs,' he said.

I dropped to my knees and inspected the dry mud floor under the planks. Dark brown insects about a fifth of an inch long, thin and flat, were scuttling towards two long cracks in the ground. Marcellin kicked the bed again, and another brittle dusting fell to the floor. 'Bedbugs,' he said. 'Their bites don't bother me.'

So this is it, I thought, my own secret fear, much more real than the idea of a Boha dagger in a kidney, and I tried to remember just where I had read that bedbugs carry the HIV virus for exactly one hour in their blood-sacs: it explains how three-year-olds and grandmothers pick it up. The bugs, sick with disappointment when their host gets out of bed, exude a drop of blood from their proboscidean hypodermic needle on the end of their noses, and then, sick with excitement, they throw up another drop as they reinsert their bloodsuckers into whoever is left between the sheets. The words of the consultant in tropical medicine at the Radcliffe hospital in Oxford came back to me: 'The Congo is *very* interesting,' he had said, with a dreamy look in his eyes. 'Very interesting indeed. It's the HIV1 and HIV2 overlap zone. If only you could send me some fresh blood samples. I'd be most grateful. I really would.'

'Marcellin,' I said, unsteadily, wondering how many women he had slept with in his hyperactive life—five hundred? a thousand?—'why don't you sleep in here? I'll sleep in the back room. And Manou and Nzé can sleep together as usual.'

Marcellin shouted, as if I were fifty yards away. 'They'll push a spear through the window in the night. I don't want to die alone! Only a coward would let me die alone! And besides,' he added, starting to calm down, 'it's all your fault. But for you I would never have returned to Boha. Never.'

'You'll thank me,' I said, momentarily hating the sight of him, and wondering why his weeping leg ulcers never quite healed despite my treating him with two courses of Floxapen. 'This is the expedition when we find your dinosaur. We'll take its portrait.'

Marcellin sat down on the edge of the bed and held his knees. 'Sleeping with you is my protection. Everyone knows there's terrible trouble when you kill a white man. With you, I'm safe. It's not right, but there it is.' He shrugged his shoulders and looked up at me with a helpless smile.

'Of course I'll sleep next to you,' I said, ashamed of myself. 'I'll sleep nearest the window.'

Well, I thought, bedbugs feed just before dawn. I'll get up at four in the morning.

There was a bang at the door. Marcellin jumped to his feet.

'Fuck off!' sang Nzé and Manou in unison.

The Vice-President appeared in the doorway, very self-effacing. 'My sister has malaria,' he said.

I counted fifteen quinine pills into his palm. 'Now,' he said, 'the Chief is waiting. He will see you now. You will follow me.'

We walked up the wide main street and stopped at a rough square on the right. In front of us was a long, windowless hut of wattle-and-daub and palm-thatch. In its doorway, on a three-legged stool, sat the Chief of Boha.

He was much younger than I had expected, perhaps in his late thirties, a handsome man of strong features, with a neatly cut moustache. He wore a thick band of red paint across his forehead, a baggy ochre loincloth with embroidered flowers over his genitals and a pair of Adidas running shoes. He held a spear upright against his right thigh, and from his shoulder hung a large twine bag full, I presumed, of the royal fetishes. He looked at us solemnly, without moving.

A yellow dog lay asleep at his feet.

Twelve spear-men stood in a circle around him and three chairs, towards which an old man in red plastic sandals tilted his spear, indicating that we were to be seated. He then pointed his spear at Nzé, motioning him away to a group of women and children who stood watching at the far side of the square. We took our places, and the circle of spear-men closed in behind us.

The Chief inclined his head to the old man, his *porte-parole*, his word-carrier, and spoke softly. The old man then straightened his back, strode into the centre of the circle, and sang out a speech in Bomitaba. At the end of the pronouncement, there were shouts from some of the spear-men and the people around the square. When the old man wanted one of them to speak he tipped his spear; and when he wanted them to stop he held it horizontally, to bar their words. The debate concluded, he returned to the Chief's side, took his instructions and returned to the centre.

'The white man will pay 75,000 francs to the Chief of Boha,' he shouted in French, 'and 20,000 francs to the Vice-President of the People's Committee. Then if the government come with soldiers to take our Chief to prison in Epéna the soldiers will have to take their own Vice-President away, too. The white men will keep faith with our customary rights.'

'It's far too much!' I said.

The old man nodded. The warrior at my back pricked me gently between the shoulder blades with his spear.

'It's a bargain!' I said.

The old man smiled, bowed his head and waved two spear-men forward to collect the presents. The Chief, without ceremony, bent forward and put the knife, the pipe and the tobacco into his shoulder-bag. He stooped down to gather up the shoes and the bolt of cloth and disappeared through the dark doorway. The old man picked up the stool and followed him inside. The royal dog lay undisturbed, his tail twitching.

3

By the time I returned to the hut, it was already full of candle-light and laughter, women and food. 'Uncle!' shouted Nzé to me, happy and sweating, standing by the table. 'Palm wine!' He passed me a mug. '*Saka-saka!*' He nodded imperiously at an old woman who was ladling mashed manioc leaves and scraps of fish from her cooking-pot. 'Pineapples!' Four were on the table, with two ripe papayas. 'Women!' He put his arm round an enormous girl sitting on his right. She looked up at me and giggled, her bright yellow and green wraparound barely restraining her breasts, her buttocks overflowing the chair. 'She's rich!' he yelled, over-excited, his wink a chaotic crush of his right eyebrow. 'Her father's a boatman! He goes to Epéna! She's well fed, Uncle!'—he squeezed the flesh of her upper arm. 'When I take her, I'll have two women at once!

'Manou!' shouted Nzé with redoubled force. 'Manou! I almost forgot. I found you a woman. Look!' He pointed into the far corner, where a young girl sat clutching a mug of palm wine, staring at her knees. She glanced at Manou, smiled and looked away. Manou sat down by the door, embarrassed. Everybody laughed.

Marcellin took me aside. 'Come on, Redmond,' he said. 'Let's leave them. Let's go and see Old Bobé. You always want to talk to old men. He knows the history of Boha. And it was he who sent us the food tonight.'

Bobé, still wearing his red-and-white-striped pyjama top, a lantern at his feet, was waiting for us in his lean-to, beneath his hunting-nets, wicker fish-traps, carrying-baskets and bundles of gourd water-containers slung from the beams.

'Welcome!' he said, jumping to his feet and shaking hands. 'You are welcome to my house.'

Bobé ushered us into armchairs grouped round a low table. Spiral horns of the swamp antelope, the sitatunga, were stuck into the plaster round the walls. A tall drum stood on its three legs in the corner, next to Marcellin.

'Bobé made this,' he said, running a finger down its side, over the joins where the different cylinders of hollowed-out tree trunks had been fitted together.

'I made everything here,' said Bobé with a slow smile, showing a full set of front teeth. 'The chairs, the table, everything.'

His wife put three empty cans labelled NORWEGIAN MACKEREL on the table, handed Bobé a gourd of palm wine and withdrew. Bobé filled the cans in silence. We picked the insects out of the white froth on top, dabbed them on to the floor and drank.

'Me, I like to be old,' said Bobé, sitting back in his chair, 'I used to be the greatest hunter in all Boha. I knew the best places to sink my fish-traps, too. But now I am old and wise. I am proud that I understand the history of my people. I know all our stories. My grandchildren and all the boys in Boha come to see me, and I tell them how it used to be. I tell them about the *colons*, the French people, and how the communists helped us to build our school. I tell them where to hunt. They like old Bobé.'

'Perhaps you could tell us about the history of your people.'

'You may talk properly,' said Marcellin to Bobé. 'He is a white man, but he respects the old ways. He has agreed to pay the traditional dues in full.'

'So I have heard,' said Bobé, turning to me, 'and you have entrusted yourself to my son Doubla, who will be your guide tomorrow. Well, we have a long history.'

He refocused his eyes to a point somewhere on the floor just behind the drum, and the hesitant old man's voice became a low incantation. He told us how the first people of Boha came from the village of Bongoye, near the plain of Sakoua, and of the path that connects the village to Lac Télé. He told us how the people moved to make the village of Bombolo, and later the village of Ngouamounkale, which also became known as Old Boha. He told us of the first chiefs and of the sorcerers and their dreams.

'So where do we all come from?' I said, pleased with myself. 'That's what I want to know. What's the origin of life?'

'That's very simple,' he said, leaning forward, refilling our ex-mackerel cans, handing me the gourd of palm wine and relaxing back into his chair, 'I can put your mind at rest. The origin of life reposes in a symbol whose name is Bolo. Bolo incarnates all creative power. It is a unique symbol. This symbol embodies all the spirits, good or bad. The origin of sorcery comes from the symbol Bolo. This symbol endows certain people with a power, a power which is generally transmitted through dreams.'

Bobé drained his second can of palm wine, refilled it—and with the can in his right hand, half-way to his lips, stopped, apparently mesmerized by something just behind the drum.

'Bobé, my old friend,' said Marcellin softly, 'we're here. Are you all right?'

'Yes, Marcellin,' he said slowly, confused. He put his can down unsteadily on the edge of the table. 'I am all right. I was listening. There is something I must tell you.

'We have come to know,' announced Bobé, intoning again, his eyes glazed over, 'that an animal of mystery lives in the forest of Boha. This animal, which is called Yombé, resembles the chimpanzee and the gorilla but its upper limbs are very elongated. It is vegetarian, and above all else it eats two species of plants which are present in our forest. This animal has already been seen on many occasions, but its mystery lies in this: you must never look into its eyes. Ten years ago, two hunters from the village shot at one of these animals, not with an arrow but with a gun. The animal, which was sitting in a tree, fell, and it disappeared, leaving not the slightest trace. The two men returned to tell their story, but as they finished speaking they were struck down. The men died.

'I, the Bobé who sits before you, affirm, now, that I too have seen this animal. I, also, met it when it was sitting in a tree. The animal began to turn its head. But the spirits of the two hunters saved my life. They called to me gently, inside my skull, and I remembered how they told their story and died. I lowered my eyes to the path. I returned to my wife and my children. So I, Bobé, I am still alive. And now I have warned you in my own house, Mister Redmond, because you are said to respect our traditions, and also because you are well known to my friend Doctor Marcellin. I warn you, on pain of death, do not meet the eye of this animal when you come across it in the forest.'

He pressed the palms of his loose-skinned old hands into his eyes, as if to shut something from view, and then looked at us with his slow smile again. 'I am tired,' he said. 'It takes courage to talk of such things. And now I am very tired. We will speak again. Perhaps you will visit me again.'

I was surprised to see that I was still holding the gourd.

'What did you make of that?' I said, as we walked back to our hut.

A stray dog appeared out of the shadows and trotted along behind us. Whenever I looked round and said

'Pheasants!', it wagged its tail and cocked its ears.

'I think you ought to know,' said Marcellin, 'that in Lingala, *Bolo* means vagina.'

I laughed.

'So why is that funny?' he said, rounding on me.

'I'm sorry,' I said, shocked at the venom in his voice. The happy pace of my walk involuntarily slowed to a shuffle. 'I thought you meant that Old Bobé was making a fool of me.'

'Oh no you didn't,' snapped Marcellin, slowing his stride to match mine, 'that's not why you laughed. Why the hell should Old Bobé want to make a fool of you? Didn't you see how tired it made him? *It's dangerous for him to talk like that.* Didn't you see how afraid he was? And then you laugh. How dare you laugh at Old Bobé!

'And anyway,' he shouted, kicking a lump of mud off the path, 'it makes as much sense as your white man's superstitions! What about your little crosses, or those beads you finger in your pockets? What about your unspeakable rites and cannibal symbols? Tell me: do you or do you not eat and drink the body and blood of the big white chief of your tribe once every seven days? Oh no—you've no right to laugh at us, at Old Bobé, at Africans.'

'I apologize. And anyway, I've told you, I'm not a Christian. I don't believe it. I don't wear a crucifix and I've never said a rosary in my life.'

'Said a rosary!' mimicked Marcellin with a yap of laughter. 'You have your little words to disguise it all, don't you? For us you say it's a fetish or a ju-ju or a gris-gris, but for you, oh yes, it's very dignified.'

'I've told you. I don't believe it.'

'Believe it or not, my friend, it's in your head. You think it's normal. You call it part of your culture. You think you're a people of reason and science, that the daylight belongs to the white man and the night to the African. And I agree, you make motor-cars and outboards and airplanes, and we don't. But what about your three gods in one, your big holy ghost that can go anywhere? Or the evil animal with feet like a goat and a long tail that divides into two at the end? Tell me, why sneer at the

African? And what about your other god who became a man and let himself be stuck on a piece of wood and speared so that he could save you all? What could it possibly mean? Where's the sense in it?'

'There is no sense in it. It's a matter of faith. Faith means saying goodbye to reason and science, that's what faith is. When you get faith you throw the switches, blow a gasket, go deliberately soft in the head. It's more comfortable.'

Marcellin ignored me.

'No wonder we were frightened of the white man when he came here with his guns and killed us and talked about eating his god all day long. We thought you were cannibals. And there's another thing—your god who never had a woman. Look—he shone the torch on his arm—'I'm the blackest African I know, with a strong need for sex. It's genetic; it's in the skin. I think about it all the time. If I don't have a woman every night I get ill. I'm ill now. You should pay me double for making me risk my life in these forests with these people. And then you should pay me double again for making me sleep in a tent without a woman at night. And for months on end! You white men, we don't know how you breed. You have a god born without any sex! And then he never had a woman! And what about the god's mother—a woman who never had a man? If that's not plain silly, I don't know what is.'

A fierce drumming began suddenly, from the far end of the village.

Marcellin was silent. Then: 'Love your neighbour as yourself,' he said, his torch beam waving wildly off the path and into the cactus hedges.

'Love your neighbour as yourself! What hypocrites!' His voice rose to its highest pitch, a falsetto shriek of indignation, of real temper. The dog turned and bolted.

'Love your neighbour! You white men burned all the Jews, just in a year or two, a mere six million. You say that was a great crime, and so it was, but what about us? What about our holocaust? From the Congo alone you sold thirteen million of us

Opposite: Doctor Marcellin Agnana.

into slavery. It went on for centuries. For centuries no man knew if he'd live to see his children grow up. What kind of god let you torture us like that?'

We entered the hut, in silence. Our guides had gone; the candles had guttered out on the table; there was nothing left in the mess tins or the bucket of palm wine. Cigarette butts were strewn over the mud floor. Nzé and Manou had hung tarpaulins flat across the doorways of the two small bedrooms.

'Oh I can't stand it here,' said Marcellin, spinning round where he stood. 'I am angry with you and your kind. I'm going to sleep at Bobé's hut.' And he picked up his pack and went.

'Psst!' said Nzé, from behind his curtain. 'Has he gone?'

'Yes, he has. He's not happy with me.'

'Well, I'm *very* happy with you,' came the whisper. 'That was the best 500 francs you ever spent on me.'

'How's that?'

'Put your head round the new bedroom door, Uncle. Just take a look at this.'

I put my head round the curtain.

'Isn't she wonderful?' said Nzé, full of pride, beaming, his towel over his genitals. 'I tell you, Uncle, she's as juicy as a ripe papaya. *She's better than a whole bottle of whisky.*'

The girl was asleep on the bed beneath the tarpaulin, her head on a pillow of Nzé's T-shirts, her yellow and green wraparound discarded on the floor.

'There's no end of her,' he said, gently drawing back the tarpaulin.

'I had her first in the school,' said Nzé. 'We had to go to get away from the others. She got so excited! "Calm yourself!" I had to say, "Calm yourself!"'

'Then what?'

'I brought her back here and I had her on the bed. And I'll tell you something—she says I'm the best! It's the gift my grandfather gave me! She's exhausted. I *am* the best. I tire them all out. There's nothing like it, Uncle.'

'I'm sure there isn't.'

'I'm going to wake her up in a minute. We're going to the dance. And then I'll have her again! Are you coming Uncle? Are you coming to the dance?'

'No, I'm not. Not tonight. I'm going for a swim, and then I'm going to bed.'

I went to the back room and found my mould-covered towel and the remains of a bar of soap, and walked down to the river by the nearest path.

Frogs quacked along the bank, and I found the washing place, took off my boots, placed my glasses gently in the left boot and my torch in the right, stripped, laid my clothes on top of the boots and waded in. To see a dinosaur suddenly seemed such a sensible western achievement: how scientific it would be to record a small sauropod from the Cretaceous. And there must be *something* odd about the lake, I thought, as I smeared myself with the towel, dressed and walked slowly back to the hut in the warm night, the drumming reaching me as a soft reverberation through the river water in my ears. It is clear that Roy Mackal in his book *A Living Dinosaur?* really did think that the lake was home to a dinosaur, partly because he supposed this to be the oldest undisturbed jungle on earth, and partly because he was sure the dinosaur was the subject of pygmy reports—and pygmy reports (unless designed to frighten the Bantu) are reliable. It was persistent Bambuti pygmy descriptions, after all, that set the English colonial officer and naturalist Sir Harry Johnston on to the search that became the greatest triumph of his career, the eventual discovery of the forest giraffe, the okapi.

As I entered the hut Mackal's other conviction seemed sensible enough—that this was the oldest undisturbed jungle on earth. Even a hundred yards from the little school, the presence of the surrounding forest felt immensely ancient, rich in evolved life. It was easy to believe that this land had remained stable for sixty-five million years, or even (pushing it a bit) to agree with Mackal that 'in a region known as the Likouala, just north of the equator, lie some of the most formidable jungle swamps on the face of the globe . . . 140,000 square kilometres of mostly unexplored swamp and rain forest.'

Nzé and his girl had gone to the dance, and Manou and his shy love had disappeared, too. I was alone in the hut. Too tired to take off my boots, I spread a tarpaulin on the planks and tried to sleep. It was no use. The voice of the Commandant echoed in my head, telling us again to stay clear of the lake, not just because we might see Mokele-mbembe but because we would certainly hear his cry, a long-drawn-out, high-pitched, echoing cry, a sound which, once heard, would deprive you of your mental balance for ever.

So thinking, I remembered the bedbugs, and, annoyed that I seemed to have lost my balance already, felt for the torch, got up, took the tarpaulin off the bed and laid it down on the mud floor. Resettled in the darkness, a stray remark of C. D. Darlington's in *The Evolution of Man and Society* rose out of my unconscious: 'Africa, the oldest home of man, is the home of the most dangerous of man's diseases.' And he was only thinking of polio, diphtheria, encephalitis I and II, leprosy, yellow fever, pneumonia, bilharzia, sleeping sickness, gonorrhoea and malaria. Which put me in mind of the Congo floor maggot.

While the tumbu fly is *quite* closely adapted to man's habits, it will also go for rats, cats, dogs and monkeys. The female lays her eggs in soil contaminated with urine or excreta or on clothes hung up to dry, so that when the tiny larvae hatch, they can burrow into the skin, producing boil-like swellings with a small, dark, moist opening near the top (their air-hole). The tumbu fly's nearest relative, the Congo floor maggot, on the other hand, is a loyal maggot, attentive only to ourselves. The female fly lays her eggs in the dust on hut floors, and at night they wriggle out and suck your blood.

As far as I knew Congo floor maggots carried no disease; they were blameless as leeches. But what, I thought, sitting up, switching on the torch and inspecting my bare arms for dangling white larvae clamped in between the hairs, if no one had bothered to check?

You're a fraud, I told myself. You've been suppressing your fear all day; that's why you're going mad. If you'd done the sensible thing when you first saw that giant with the knife who wanted to kill Marcellin—if you'd just sat down on the path and howled—you'd be sleeping like a bushpig. And if there is a small chance that HIV can be spread in the malaria parasite, and if there is a very big chance that it is carried by bedbugs (known also to transmit hepatitis B), what one-hundred-per-cent hunk of a chance is there that it's also inside a Congo floor maggot?

'In any case,' I said aloud, as I got up and spread my tarpaulin back on the bed again, 'I'd rather be bitten by a bug than sucked by a maggot. And there's nothing mad about that. In fact it's perfectly normal'—I took off my boots—'no sane man wants a maggot in his bed. But bugs, there's nothing you can do about them.'

So I lay on the planks and tried to think of something peaceful: of the little bedroom in the Wiltshire vicarage of my childhood; of the blackbird which used to perch each summer evening on the roof of the bicycle shed below my window and sing me to sleep; of the wood-pigeons in the conker tree. But it didn't work. Nothing held for long enough; my brain was too disturbed to be directed in its dreams; my imagination obstinately filled with thoughts of Bruce Chatwin, the only person I knew who had died of AIDS.

'Redders!' would come a familiar voice down the phone far too early in the morning. 'Not even Bunin was interesting yesterday. I can't stand it a moment longer.

'I'm sick of writing. I'm tired! Tired! Tired!' (said with enough energy to crack your ear-drum). 'And when a man is sick of writing he must walk.' (*Oh god.*) 'I'm coming to get you.' (*Panic.*) 'What are you doing?'

'I'm in bed.'

'Up you get! Two glasses of green tea. See you in half an hour.'

I wondered who or what Bunin was. With Bruce you could never be sure. The new Stravinsky from Albania? The nickname of the last slave in Central Mali? A lighthouse keeper from Patagonia? Scroll 238B from a cave in the Negev? Or just the *émigré* king of Tomsk who'd dropped in for tea? Still vaguely wondering, I lurched out of the house.

A white 2CV puttered into the drive. There was a sailboard strapped to the roof. Chatwin got out, his wife Elizabeth's two

45

dogs wagging at his feet.

'Come on! It's almost dawn! I'm taking these brutes to a hill-farm in Wales. We'll look at the tree of life on the south door of St Mary and St David at Kilpeck; we'll deliver the dogs; we'll call in on my old friend Lady Betjeman; and then I'll walk you over the Black Hill.'

'So what's the sailboard for?' I said, suspicious.

'Oh that. That's my new hobby. You bring your car and make your own way back tonight, and I'll go sailing in the Bristol Channel in the morning.'

And you'll probably be in Dublin for supper, I thought.

Beneath the first ridge of the Black Mountains we parked by a track and got out our boots: mine, black Wellingtons; his, a pair of such fine leather that Hermès would have done a swap. I put on my bergen (a loaf of bread and two bottles of wine) and he put on his small haversack of dark maroon calfskin (a Montblanc pen, a black oilcloth-bound *vrai* moleskin notebook, a copy of Alymer Maude's translation of *War and Peace*, Strindberg's *By the Open Sea* and the most elegant pair of binoculars I have seen).

'Werner Herzog gave them to me,' said Bruce, his eyes blue and bright and eager. 'He wants to film *The Viceroy of Ouidah*. And Jean-Louis Barrault had this pack designed just for me. But you *could* get some decent boots, Redders. The Canadian Moccasin Company. Just say you're a friend of mine.'

He took off up the hill with a strong, loping stride through the heather and the whinberries, a nomad's pace. In a few minutes I fell behind, trying not to pant like an engine shed.

'The twins I wrote about lived there,' he said, turning without slackening and pointing to a long slate-roofed farmhouse set back from the road in the diminishing valley below us.

'And . . . that's . . . where!!!' His words whipped past me, split up and lost to sense in the wind. The speed of ascent was effort enough, replying to the wild and ceaseless monologue an impossibility—which was just as well, because it was far too late in our friendship to admit that, much as I admired *In Patagonia*, what with one siesta and another I had just not quite read *On the Black Hill*.

'There's a hippie camp down there,' he called, nodding

north-west. He shouted with laughter. 'All the locals are terrified of them. They think they'll be strangled in their beds! When I was staying with the King of Afghanistan he had an old English colonel about the court. "Your Royal Highness," said the colonel, "You must let me remove all the hips from your country. You must let me put all the hips in trucks and take them to the border."'

Down on the Llanthony road, we walked through the hail, and Bruce talked about a female albatross that had wandered into the wrong hemisphere and built a nest in Shetland, waiting for the mate that never came, and about the train he caught from King's Cross on his way to see her, and how the only other passenger in his sleeper compartment was a Tierra del Fuegan ('On his way to the North Sea oil rigs—they're the only men who can throw a boat's painter through a ring on a buoy') whose settlement Bruce had visited on the journey that became *In Patagonia*.

He talked about his love for the herd-people of the Sudan; about smuggling Roman coins out of Turkey; about the design of a prehistoric wheel which linked the Irish to an ethnic sub-group in the Caucasus (I think); and about his real dream, the Russian novel he would write one day.

There was the noise of an engine shaking itself to bits, three violent backfires, and a rust-holed van lurched up the road towards us. I jumped on to the bank at the base of the hedge, but Bruce, engrossed, was still walking in the road. Surprisingly slowly, it seemed, the van nudged the Jean-Louis Barrault haversack and, equally slowly, Bruce, still talking ('Just tell the story straight as Tolstoy. No tricks!'), turned a full somersault in the air.

'You stupid bastards!' shouted Bruce, getting to his feet. 'That was unnecessary.'

A young boy, his hair in a pony-tail, jumped down from the cab. 'Sorry, squire,' he said, 'I'm sorry. Honest. What more can I say? It's like this—my wheels hasn't got no brakes.'

'I say,' said Bruce. 'How exciting. Can we have a lift?'

Just back from months in the jungle between the Orinoco and the Amazon, I thought I'd celebrate with warm scallops in a London restaurant and got a six-month dose of hepatitis A. Half-asleep, eyes shut in the isolation wing of the Churchill Hospital in Oxford, I heard a familiar voice.

'Shush,' it said, 'don't tell anyone. I'm not here.'

I opened one eye. So it was true. Hepatitis A induced delirium. You saw visions on it.

'Shush, I'm in France. Bill Buford's after me. I'm meant to be writing a piece for *Granta*. I'm not here. But with you here too I might just as well phone Reuters and be done with it.

'I've brought you some liver pills. They're from Elizabeth's guru in India. I'm having aboriginal warts removed from my face. I'm in the room next door. Look, will you be my literary executor? I'll do the same for you if you die first.'

'I'll do anything you say. I want to go to sleep.'

'You know, there's something else I want you to know. When I first came in here they told me I was mortally ill. They said I had a fungus of the bone marrow which I must have picked up in a cave in China. It's exclusive! It's so rare that I'm only the tenth recorded case in the medical literature! And they also let me know why I got it, Redders. I got it because I have AIDS. They told me I had six months or a year to live. So I thought, right, Bruce is a dog's name and I'm not going to stand for this. I can't get on with my big nomad book as it is. I can't see how I can pull material out of my notebooks and on to the page. And I'm not going to waste away and go feeble in the head and defecate all over the place.

'So I went to Geneva—there's a place in the Alps that haunts me, a ravishing cliff near Jungfrau—and I wanted to jump off it. Or, failing that, I thought I'd go to Niger and simply take off my clothes, put on my loincloth, walk out into the desert and let the sun bleach me away.

'But the bone marrow got me first. I fainted on the pavement; someone took me to hospital in a taxi; and Elizabeth came and rescued me and brought me back here. I was so weak I couldn't whisper. I came in on a Friday and they thought I'd be dead by Monday. Then Juel-Jensen put me on his anti-fungal drip, and Elizabeth nursed me night and day, and I pulled through: I owe it all to them.

'I've almost finished my big book—there's a terrible old

character with a twisted gut called Hanlon—and now I have a
whole novel growing in the notebooks, too. I can see almost all
of it. It's set in Prague and I shall call it "Utz"—"Utz"! Anyway,
one day you must tell people, Redders, but not now. It's a fable.
It's all there, ready-made. And the moral is simple: never kill
yourself. Not under any circumstances. Not even when you're
told you have AIDS.'

I last saw Bruce in Elizabeth's light-filled house which looks
south down an Oxfordshire valley; he was in his second bedroom,
books on the counterpane, the manuscript of a young novelist he
had befriended and encouraged stacked in a box by the bed,
cassettes of young musicians he had supported piled on the
bedside table, his newly bought Russian icons on the walls.

Though he was very weak and so thin you could see the
white bones in his arms, his telephone was still plugged into its
socket. He was making and receiving calls, talking to his friends
all over the world.

'Just for now, Redders, I can't hold a pen. It would be
ridiculous to start yet, and I hate dictation. But the moment I'm
better I'll begin that Russian novel. It's going to work. I can see
almost all of it. No tricks!'

His grin gave out in a burst of coughing. As I left, the sun
bright on the walls, I took his hands in both of mine. A thought
struck him, and he gave a snort of laughter.

'Redders! Your hands—they're so soft I don't believe you
ever go anywhere. You just lie in bed and make it all up.'

They were his last words to me. And quite right, too, I
thought. I must read Bunin. And get a sailboard.

But it won't be the same.

A loud clank up under the corrugated-iron roof brought me
back to full consciousness. With disbelief I remembered
exactly where I was, and then someone screamed outside.
Something hit the bed and scratched against my arm. Jesus, I
thought, sliding sideways and grabbing the torch from the top of
the bergen. *It's a spear through the shutter.* And I snapped on the
light.

From the head of the bed, an enormous, fluffy, white-bellied, grey-backed rat looked at me, frozen, his eyes as wide as mine, his cheeks puffed out, his ears forward, shaped like spoons, his tail white at the end and much too long. We stared at each other, both of us hyperventilating; the fur over his rib-cage pumped in and out; my heart twitched like a dislodged ball of maggots in my chest.

'It's OK,' I said, shaking, 'you're a rat.'

The rat, appalled by such obviousness in the middle of the night, jumped at the wall, scrabbled, fell off again, and scuttered out of the door.

'He's so clean,' I said; and then: 'You must look him up.' And then: 'You must stop talking to yourself.'

I got Theodor Haltenorth and Helmut Diller's *A Field Guide to the Mammals of Africa including Madagascar* (1977) out of my bergen. There he sat, on plate twenty-six, still startled, but with one paw up like a boxer: the giant Gambian rat.

In Africa apparently, it was not just dinosaurs that had strange habits; rats did odd things, too, even for rats. The giant Gambian rat, for instance, liked to take a shit while doing a handstand. My rat had obviously miscalculated, banged his upturned buttocks on the corrugated-iron roof and taken a header on to the bed. Unless, of course, his face looked so puffed out because he was already thinking of 'the subsidiary use of cheek pouches to collect unpalatable objects (nails, coins, bottle tops, ballpoint pens etc.) for storing in a chamber below ground.'

I was just restraining myself from checking the ballpoint pens in my bergen when someone screamed. So, by association, I looked up the dwarf bushbaby.

She stared out at me from plate forty-eight, as did the angwantibo, bigger, heavier, more thickly furred, with smaller ears and no tail. 'Penis with bone,' my Haltenorth and Diller told me, 'prepuce without horny spines, with papillae only, scrotum hairy as far as the small glandular horny surface at base. Clitoris long and thick, root-thickened and turnip-shaped; in corner of vulva a small horny plate holding a scent gland.'

The angwantibo is a relative of our ancestors, so why had we lost our penis bone? Was Richard Dawkins right, that it was as a result of so-called honest signalling, a response to selection pressure from females, the result of a woman's need to find the best possible father for her offspring? In the same way that the ribbon-tail bird of paradise (for instance) displays his absurdly long white tail (a real handicap in normal life) to show the girls (perhaps) that he is not suffering from diarrhoea and so is free of parasites, a man who can pump up his penis with blood demonstrates that he is well-fed, free of stress and disease and only mildly kinky. Whereas any old man can wave a bone about. I thought it was an ingenious, thoroughly pleasing idea—until I also thought what a disadvantage it would be to have a long white tail round here, given the speed with which manioc went through the system, and that if I was to do a spot of honest signalling myself right then there would be no doubt about the message: abject fear.

It was all too much at last. I fell asleep.

4

I woke well after dawn, covered in small red bites, and went for a swim to calm the all-over itch. When I returned Manou was up, moving at twice his normal speed, his eyes bright.

'She likes me,' he said.

'Of course she does. She knows how strong you are, how fast you're going to walk in the forest.'

'It wasn't like that,' said Manou with a proud little smile, 'she said she loved my body. And my hat.'

Nzé emerged from behind his curtain; he held on to the edge of the table, as though he had just suffered a mild blow to the back of the head. 'She's gone to her mother,' he mumbled. 'She's gone to sleep at her mother's house. She kept screaming, Uncle. Every time. She begged me to stop. She said, Nzé, that was the best night of my life, and I said, Yes, you big bag of happiness, for me that was the best time I've ever had at a school desk.'

Marcellin, looking grim, arrived with our new guides, Doubla (because of his double character) and Vicky (the Chief's favourite son). 'What are you doing?' Marcellin shouted at Manou and Nzé. 'Why aren't you ready? Why aren't the loads outside the hut? The bearers are here.'

We pushed everything into the bergens and lined them up against the hut wall. Doubla and Vicky, I noticed, had come barefoot. 'Shoes are precious here,' said Marcellin. 'No one wears them in the forest.'

Nzé fired his gun into the air to mark our departure. The African grey parrots shrieked and swore somewhere off to our right.

We were on the move again, beneath the familiar trees, away from the insistent press of village life. For me, every time we entered the jungle, it seemed like an escape; Marcellin felt it very differently. For him, as he wrote and underlined in his diary which I was secretly reading whenever I got the chance, '*Setting out into the forest is like a soldier going to war, the return is never certain.*'

What was he so afraid of—a leopard? disease? snakebite? breaking a leg? Or was there, underneath all that Cuban Marxist education in Havana, all that French pharmacy and biology at Montpellier, just a trace of suppressed terror? Did he half share his sorcerer-grandfather's belief in the power of fetish? Was he so tense simply because he thought this particularly malign stretch of forest was haunted by spirit animals? Or maybe, I thought, Marcellin just suspects that Doubla and the brothers have secret instructions to murder us in the forest.

Vicky led the way and I followed, trying to match his stride: his bare feet slapped easily over the ground with fast, small steps—the only way to walk at speed, I now knew, without sliding across the dank scatter of leaves on the wet mud. Getting vaguely into the rhythm, the sweat oozing down my face in the humid, unmoving air, I fell into a trance. It was only really possible to be alone in Africa, it occurred to me, when walking like this, or when awake on a tarpaulin in the middle of the night: anyone on his own was in danger, an isolated man was an easy prey for wandering spirits, friends must keep together always, and talk.

The great trees towered above us, their sixty-foot-high trunks not even tapering until they reached the canopy, where their massive branches spread out horizontally. Lianas looped and sagged in spirals along their branches; ferns and epiphytic orchids grew whenever plant debris had lodged in their high forks; and every surface was patched with lichens. But it was not a dense forest. We passed many gaps in the high canopy and some of the smaller trees had prop roots. But there were very few bushes and herbs in the understory, and even the broad-leaved grasses were sparse. We were well on our way towards swamp jungle.

Vicky suddenly stopped, leaned his spear against a sapling, eased himself out of the bergen and bent down to pick up yellow, cooking-apple-sized fruits which were scattered over the path.

'Gorillas and chimpanzees like them,' he said, grinning at me, a super-signal of white teeth across his wide, brown, sweaty, happy face. 'You try one.'

He took his machete, cut the top off the fruit like an egg, gave it to me, and selected another for himself; under the wrinkled yellow skin a cup of orange flesh enclosed a ball of white fluff. Vicky scooped it out, discarding a cluster of big brown seeds, and I copied him, gathering a mouthful of sweetish floss.

'Mokele-mbembe,' said Vicky, mysteriously, and winked.

'Malombo,' said Marcellin, coming up behind me. The others arrived and everyone began to eat.

Malombo, according to Roy Mackal, is the main food plant of Mokele-mbembe, and I half expected a brown, skin-flappy sauropod head on its giraffe-length neck to come slithering over my shoulder and muzzle up my fruit. (Would its lips be cold, I wondered, or were the dinosaurs really warm-blooded?) Or at the very least we might hear the high-pitched ululating cry that would drive us all berserk.

The forest grew wetter, prop-rooted trees more common, and we heard the alarm-calls of greater white-nosed monkeys. The men of Boha were gossiping loudly in Bomitaba; Nzé was shouting tales of Dongou in Lingala to Marcellin; and Manou was too busy conserving his strength to say anything at all. We saw little: the occasional pile of fibrous grey lowland-gorilla turds, clumps of wild ginger and strands of some kind of arrowroot, a herb with gigantic leaves borne on single stems six to eight feet high. We stopped, finally, to examine a line of fresh, elongated rat-like droppings.

Doubla said they were mongoose turds, so I got Haltenorth and Diller's guide from the side pocket of the bergen. Doubla inspected all the possible snouts, feet, thick coats and long furry tails of the twenty-seven mongooses illustrated on plates thirty-three to thirty-seven and chose the marsh mongoose.

The marsh mongoose was plainly an emotional mongoose ('VOICE: purrs when content; in threat or defence, growls, nasal snorting and spitting; in excitement, a staccato rising bark; with fluffing up of fur expressing rage'), but the details of its breeding and development were not known. This was promising. And what's more (apart from the lack of a light yellow rim to its ears) it looked exactly like the *extremely* rare long-nosed mongoose, also reported from the northern Congo swamp forest—a mongoose whose 'teats, glands and penis bone' were *still* undescribed, and of whom 'only 30 specimens known . . . No details of habits.'

'So why not this one?' I said, getting excited, pointing at the illustration. 'Look—*only thirty specimens known.*'

'Why not?' said Doubla, shrugging his shoulders, 'if that's what you want.'

'But, Redmond,' said Marcellin, bristling, picking up the turd between two fingers. 'I am a scientist and I tell you—it's not likely is it? *All we have here is a piece of shit!*'

OK, I was on the verge of saying, as I put the book back in its pocket, as far as your Mokele-mbembe is concerned you don't even have a piece of shit, do you? And, come to that, I'll bet a decent dinosaur turd is something we could really feast our eyes on. In fact I'd settle for one-eighth of a dingleberry hanging off its bum. Or an absolutely genuine sauropod snot. Or a toe-nail clipping. Or even a discarded fag-butt. If it's not too much to ask.

I thought of the hard time that Mokele-mbembe must have had in the last sixty-seven million years.

In his book, Roy Mackal tells us:

One of the most exciting things about Africa is that, at least since the end of the Cretaceous period, 65 million years ago, the Congo basin has not undergone further climatic and geophysical changes . . . When conditions remain stable for extended periods, some well-adapted species continue to survive and even flourish with very little physical and behavioural alteration. And that is what we find in the central West African jungle-swamps where, for example, crocodiles have persisted unchanged over the past 65 million years. What other ancient creatures might still lurk in this vast expanse of seemingly changeless, ageless, largely unexplored primeval forest?

In fact if we go back to the beginning, from Mokele-mbembe's point of view, I thought, getting excited, taking a sleepwalker's swig from my water-bottle and almost running into the back of Vicky's spear, then Mackal's case—resting on the assumption that the jungle here has not been disturbed—becomes even more convincing. The sauropods evolved 225 million years ago, and if Mokele-mbembe's ancestors were in Lac Télé or thereabouts for the next few million years, then, apart from that very bad moment sixty-seven million years ago when an incoming meteorite six miles across blasted pulverized rock into the atmosphere and greenhoused all other large dinosaurs to oblivion, they might have had the odd minor, nasty surprise over their breakfast as the sea came rolling in, once or twice. We can picture them in the late Cretaceous, seventy-two million years ago, basking with their Loch Ness necks and little heads and humpbacks out of the water, surrounded by recognizable plants and recognizable birds: gulls, ducks, waders and herons. There were snakes about, as well as frogs, salamanders and of course freshwater crocodiles. And for Mokele-mbembe, life went peacefully by until about six million years ago, when the Congo basin filled into a giant lake. The relics of that vast lake were all about us: the swamp forest, the Oubangui and Congo rivers, the shallow lakes and, perhaps, Lac Télé itself, just one day's walk away.

There was a swish of wings like a quetzacoatlus overhead, a call like the braying of dinosaurs—and a pair of black-casqued hornbills returned me to the present. As big as cormorants, they were perched high up on a branch to our right, their great bills swaying from side to side, peering down at us.

Redmond O'Hanlon

We made camp in a tiny clearing off the path, beside the black patch of an old cooking fire whose ashes glinted with mother-of-pearl—scales from the undersides of the forest crocodile. Hundreds of bees and four species of butterflies were feeding round its edge.

Doubla and Vicky cut poles from saplings and set up a shelter with our tarpaulins on one side of the clearing. And as Marcellin and I pitched our tents on the other, the feeding bees transferred their attentions to us. They settled on our sweat-soaked shirts and crawled down our chests and necks; they clustered in our armpits. They were joined by clouds of black bees, who buzzed around our faces and made their way into our hair, sucking at the corners of our eyes and mouths and at the mucus in our noses and the wax in our ears. We took off our shirts and hung them near the fire, cut switches and then tried not to let our arms touch our sides (stings in the armpit are almost as painful as stings in the crotch).

Doubla and Vicky sharpened two heavy saplings into stakes, enlarged the muddy pit of a water-hole and filled Nzé's cooking-pot. The light failed and the bees left, and Nzé slopped sour manioc stodge and two sardines apiece into our mess-tins. We sat on our different tree-roots round the fire and ate in silence.

'Cheer up!' said Nzé finally, pulling a small gourd of palm-wine from his food-sack. 'Let's have a last drink, because in a day or two, when we get to Lac Télé, anything may happen. I'll tell you what I'm going to do—I'm going to shoot myself a Mokele-mbembe. In fact,' he paused, and inclined his head to one side, as if in deep deliberation, 'maybe I'll shoot more than one!'

'You shouldn't talk about it,' said Manou quietly. 'You don't know anything about it.'

'Oh yes I do,' said Nzé, 'and what's more I can make you laugh whenever I want to. I've got the power—so you can't help yourselves.'

He put his mug down, stood up and, turning to me with a

Opposite: Redmond O'Hanlon, his hat covered by two different kinds of bee.

56

flourish, fixed me with his good eye. 'I'm teaching Redmon to speak like a man,' he said. 'I'm teaching him Lingala.' He leaned forward and wagged a finger in my face, as though I were a child. 'I WANT SOME FOOD,' he shouted, '*MAKATA ELLOKO MOLOMOU.*'

'*Makata*,' I repeated dutifully, '*elloko molomou.*'

Everyone howled with laughter. Even Doubla laughed, a bark of horrible energy.

'Nzé, that's enough,' said Marcellin, regaining his dignity. 'What if he said that in a village? Eh? What would people think of me?

'Redmond,' said Marcellin, 'if you really want to learn, I'll teach you Lingala myself. You can trust me. I am a scientist. "I want some food" is *Na liki ko liya biliya. Makata elloko molomou* on the other hand is what Nzé tells all the girls in all the villages. It means MY COCK IS BEAUTIFUL.'

I stretched out luxuriously on the tarpaulin in the safety of the little tent, moved my strained ankle-joints this way and that, wiggled my bruised toes, flexed my aching calf-muscles and decided that, having lost at least three stone since coming to the Congo, I was probably fitter than I'd ever been in my life. I shifted my position to avoid the roots under my shoulder-blade and was injected in the back with two small syringes of boiling water.

Cursing myself for forgetting the insect-check routine, I switched on the torch, found my glasses and squashed the two bees in the bed with Haltenorth and Diller's *Mammals of Africa*. I killed another one crawling across the sweaty webbing of my bergen and three more resting, surfeited, on the socks in my boot. I eased off my shirt and picked about with my Swiss Army knife tweezers, trying to remove the barbs; I rubbed Anthisan into the swellings, put a fresh dressing over the main ulcer on my right foot, which the day's march had re-opened, and, still waiting for the immediate pain in my back to subside, retrieved the document wallet from my pack and drew out my photocopies. Yes, here it was: Marcellin on record, as plain as could be, in the appendix to Roy Mackal s *A Living Dinosaur? In Search of*

Mokele-mbembe: in 1983, Doctor Marcellin Agnagna writes, he stayed for a week at Boha, 'the inhabitants of which "own" Lac Télé, one of the reported habitats of Mokele-mbembe.' And on 26 April

> the expedition then set out on foot, accompanied by seven villagers from Boha who were to act as guides in the forest. The trail through the forest proved to be quite difficult and it was usually necessary to cut through the foliage to allow passage. It being the dry season, water was scarce, and it became necessary to drink from muddy pools.
>
> The 60-kilometre trek to Lake Télé was completed in 2 days, and it was with some emotion that we finally looked across this little sea, located right in the heart of the equatorial forest of Central Africa. The lake is oval in shape, about 5 kilometres by 4 kilometres. A base camp was established at the water's edge, and one of the Boha villagers caught a large turtle which served as dinner that first night. Two days of intensive observing of the lake produced no sightings of the supposed Mokele-mbembe, although there were frequent observations of a large turtle, with a shell reaching 2 metres in length.
>
> On 1 May, 1983, the author decided to film the fauna in the low-canopy forest surrounding the lake. This forest is a habitat for many mammalian and bird species. The author and two Boha villagers, Jean Charles Dinkoumbou and Issac Manzamoyi, set out early in the morning. At approximately 2.30 p.m., the author was filming a troop of monkeys. One of the villagers, Dinkoumbou, fell into a pool of muddy water, and went to the edge of the lake to wash himself. About 5 minutes later, we heard his shouts to come quickly. We joined him by the lake, and he pointed to what he was observing, which was at first obscured by the heavy foliage. We were then able to observe a strange animal, with a wide back, a long neck, and a small head. The

emotion and alarm at this sudden, unexpected event disrupted the author's attempt to film the animal with a Minolta XL-42 movie camera. The film had been almost totally exposed already, and the author unfortunately began filming in the macro position. By the time this was realised, the film had been totally exposed, as determined by subsequent processing in a French laboratory.

The animal was located at about 300 metres from the edge of the lake, and we were able to advance about 60 metres in the shallow water, placing us at a distance of about 240 metres from the animal, which had become aware of our presence and was looking around as if to determine the source of the noise. Dinkoumbou continued to shout with fear. The frontal part of the animal was brown, while the back part of the neck appeared black and shone in the sunlight. The animal partly submerged, and remained visible for 20 minutes with only the neck and head above the water. It then submerged completely, at which point we trekked rapidly through the forest back to the base camp, located 2 kilometres away. We then went out on the lake in a small dugout with video equipment to the spot where we had observed the animal. However, no further sighting of the animal took place.

It can be said with certainty that the animal we saw was Mokele-mbembe, that it was quite alive, and, furthermore, that it is known to many inhabitants of the Likouala region. Its total length from head to back visible above the waterline was estimated at 5 metres.

A soft but persistent rain began to patter on the canvas. I turned off the precious batteries, lay on my side with two mould-rotted shirts under my hip and a pair of pants for a pillow and half-dreamed about Darwin's cousin, Francis Galton, pioneer geneticist and statistician, father of the anti-cyclone and fingerprinting. It was one of Galton's ostensibly more trivial experiments that filled my mind as I fell asleep. Fascinated by the so-called worship of idols, he decided to investigate its mechanism and cast around for an entirely inappropriate image. He settled on Mr Punch. He pinned a cover of the journal up in his study and forced himself to make obeisance every morning, detailing his fears, whispering his hopes, until the experiment began to work so well he had to stop. Each time he entered his club and caught a glimpse of Mr Punch lying in state on the periodicals table his mouth went dry, his legs became unsteady and a sweat broke out across his shoulders.

Here in the forest, I thought, there seemed no mystery at all about the power of Mr Punch.

5

To avoid the bees we broke camp at four-thirty and left at first light. The rain had stopped, and the forest seemed subdued. We heard little: the odd troop of mangabeys chatter-grunting; the electric swarm of bees passing overhead, late for some appointment; and the usual background calls—the prolonged, mournful *hoo-hoo-hoo* of the grey wood pigeon, from high up in the canopy of the tallest trees, and the spectral laugh of the red-billed dwarf hornbill.

Around midday, we came upon a small clearing that had been made by machete. Everyone stopped and slid off their loads.

'What's this?' I said.

'It's nothing,' said Marcellin. 'It's a piece of superstition. You stay here with us.'

Doubla stuck his spear upright in the soft ground and he and Vicky moved off in single file beyond it, up a path to our right. They stopped by an old safou tree and bowed their heads. I took off my hat, bowed my head likewise and held my hands behind my back. Vicky shouted into the bushes, the umbrella trees, pausing occasionally as he listened to the short replies of the dead.

The conversation completed, he took me by the arm. 'We can go now,' he said, with a smile. 'It is good you were here. We are pleased. I told them that we have come here to take a white man to Lac Télé and asked them to give us food and to protect us from seeing something.'

'Mokele-mbembe?'

He laughed.

'No,' said Doubla, giving the air in front of him a rabbit-chop, as if to break the neck of the question, 'you might think it was a chimpanzee or a gorilla, this something, but it's dangerous. It is not good to name names.'

'Was this your old village?'

'Yes, but they became frightened. They were frightened of strange things in this forest. There are strange sounds in this forest.'

'No more questions,' said Doubla. 'That's enough. We must not disturb them any longer.'

Marcellin was sitting on one of the surface-roots of a forest giant. 'Redmond!' he said, 'I have been thinking. If we ever get out of here alive—if the Chief of Boha really has forgiven us—then you owe me a great deal.' He began to swing his feet, kicking his heels against the side of the root. 'This is the longest expedition I have made in the forest but I have also made eight others. I have conducted a survey of the forest elephant populations in this country and I am well known in England and North America for my work on Mokele-mbembe. I am a scientist. I do not belong here. What future is there? And how about my daughter? How will she get an education? Eh? You Redmond—you must pay me back. You must get me a job in Oxford. I want to be an Oxford Professor.'

'But that's not how it works,' I said, taken aback. Perhaps *this* was Marcellin's sustaining fantasy. 'I don't have the slightest influence in Oxford,' I said. 'And even if I did, it's not as easy as you think. There aren't any jobs in England. There are two million people looking for jobs.'

'I don't believe you,' he snapped. 'I don't believe you, Redmond. You just say that. You say it because I am a black man. I understand you, my friend. Two million people! That's, that's more than the entire population of the Congo! I don't believe a word you say.'

He stopped drumming his heels on the side of the root; he

stared out beyond me, over my head, at some point in the dark tangle of shade on the far side of the clearing; he looked wistful. His shoulders seemed to collapse in on themselves, shrinking his chest; his hands hung limp over his knees. 'You could try,' he said, in a voice so small it was almost a whisper.

'There are bound to be scholarships,' I said, without conviction. 'You could probably get a grant. You could finish your doctorate.'

Marcellin looked at his feet. 'I am not a student!' he shouted, swinging off the root and drawing his machete. With one blow he severed the loop of the thick liana a foot above his head. An initial gush of water adjusted itself to an even flow as wide as a finger; he pulled the liana over his upturned mouth and drank. When he had finished Doubla followed suit, splashing the water over his head and neck, and we each took a turn.

'You see,' said Marcellin gently, 'I know about little things, too. I know which vines to drink from, and which vines will kill you.'

We set off again, with Marcellin in the lead. A little snakebite of shame spread up from the path and into my skull with the rising sweat and rhythm of his absurdly fast pace. 'You're bloated, aren't you?' went the usual refrain in my head. 'You're fat with all the unearned privilege that has come your way, with all the gross advantages that were yours for the taking just because of the country you were born in.' And I thought of the light on the ochre stone of the Bodleian quadrangle in Oxford on a summer morning, the tall mullioned windows, the books—every book a man could possibly need, ascending row after row to the high ceilings, or standing in the stacks underground, beneath the ancient paving stones and the manicured gravel, shelf-mile on mile. And I thought of Marcellin's hut of an office in Brazzaville with nothing in it but two issues of the *Journal of Cryptozoology*.

I thought of the young Marcellin and his father, who deserted his mother upriver in Impfondo and moved to the capital, living in the poorest part of the poorest quarter of the city with an open drain outside their shack; and I imagined the boy walking uptown every evening to do his homework under a street lamp, intent on winning the scholarship that would take him to Cuba. And then the path plunged waist-deep into black water, and I rapidly ceased to think of anything except the invisible submerged roots which trapped my feet and cracked my shins.

Marcellin was flailing ahead of me, hardly slackening his pace, and I was spitting out another mouthful of leaf-rot, retrieving my hat, when suddenly there were bright flashes as if someone were holding mirrors up among the trees ahead. The flashes grew together and turned into a consistent layer of light, head-high between the trunks ahead. And there in front of us was a stretch of water, three or four kilometres across. It was open water, a real horizon for the first time in months. We had reached Lac Télé.

Nzé, bedraggled, ran straight for the low bank as if to hurl himself into the water, but Doubla, with fearsome energy, lunged out and gripped his arm—so hard that Nzé yelped like a hit dog. 'Wait!' said Doubla. 'You'll harm us all. You'll kill our children.'

Vicky took a step forward, bowed his head and shouted towards the far shore. 'The spirits of the lake,' he said, turning to us, 'tell me we are welcome here.' Nzé, released, laid his gun down, lurched forward, stretched himself full-length on the low bank, cupped his hands in the water and drank like a bushpig.

We walked a little way along the shore, behind the palms and trees and lianas to a promontory where a space had been cleared: Marcellin's old camp. A tree had been felled as a makeshift jetty, and two small fishing canoes lay wedged against it, half-submerged.

'I made these here,' said Doubla, suddenly friendly. 'I made them myself.'

'Doubla! You take the gun!' shouted Marcellin, imperiously, as if he had never suspected he might be murdered. 'We need meat.'

Doubla gave a half-smile, slapped me on the back and slipped away into the jungle behind us.

Opposite: Marcellin Agnagna during the journey to Lac Télé.

The brothers began to set up a shelter, and Manou and Nzé built a fire. Marcellin pitched his tent in the only other available space, within three yards of the bank, and I put mine up beside his. No one would do this in the forests of the Amazon, I thought idly; no one would want to sleep so close to the water, not with all those anacondas about. Just suppose you were an anaconda. You'd need about two feet of body-length to anchor your tail firmly to a tree-root underwater; one foot to rear silently over the bank; nine feet to reach that warm rank mammalian smell of the tent entrance; an extra foot (at most) to slide in your rat-brown head; and then all you had to do was get a good grip on my face with your fifty or so backward-slanting pointed teeth, retract those massive muscles of yours for a second or two—and I'm safely coiled up underwater. So if you're as long as the longest anaconda recorded, at thirty-seven feet, that leaves you a good twenty-four feet to play with. And even if you're just a stolidly average sort of anaconda at around twenty feet, that still leaves you a seven-foot leeway. And, as you've been documented swallowing a six-foot cayman, you'd have no trouble swallowing me, complete with boots, glasses, camera, binoculars and a packet full of Savlon tubes. And then, how much, I wondered, does Marcellin know about pythons?

'Marcellin!' I shouted, 'are there any pythons here?'

'Pythons!' Marcellin shouted back, sticking his head out of his tent-flap, coming alive. 'I should say so! This is the best place in all Congo for pythons! Last time I was here I saw them all round the lake—just wrapped up in the trees, hanging down over the water—maybe one every five hundred yards. They were *big*, Redmond—twenty? twenty-five?—the record is thirty-two feet! They swallow leopards! They swallow *crocodiles!*'

Doubla, triumphant, returned with a blue duiker, a forest antelope about the size of a roe deer, grey-brown with a whitish belly, large black eyes and two tiny horns.

'There you are,' he said, dumping it down in front of Nzé, 'one cartridge! One *mboloko!*'

'So what?' said Nzé, hurt. 'My grandfather didn't need cartridges. He used to change himself into a leopard at night—

and in the morning we'd have bushpig to eat, whenever we wanted.'

To my surprise, nobody laughed.

Nzé set to butchering the duiker, as the men of Boha made desultory talk in Bomitaba around the fire. Marcellin sat apart on a log, his head in his hands, staring at the ground.

'It's not good,' said Marcellin suddenly. 'We've been in this forest too long, Redmond. I had a terrible dream last night. I'd just got home, and as I entered my house, my fridge—it blew up. It blew up and my baby daughter was covered in blood, and my wife was screaming, and I held my daughter in my arms until she died. Nothing will ever replace her, and there's no point to anything. It's not worth it, all this.'

'I don't think fridges blow up.'

'This one did. I have a very good fridge. I have the very latest fridge. It's made in France.'

'I had a bad dream, too,' said Nzé, squatting on his haunches, the roughly skinned, ripped-up carcass at his feet, lobbing bits of muscle, heart, spleen, liver and gut indiscriminately into the pot. 'I dreamed my cock blew up.'

'Not before time,' said Doubla.

'I got that disease again, Uncle, and your medicine was no good, and my cock couldn't stand the strain any more and so it just blew up with a whacking great bang in the middle of the night. They heard it all over Dongou. And every girl in Dongou said to herself, "*There goes my last chance of happiness.*"'

We cheered.

'It's easy to cure diseases like yours,' said Doubla. 'All you need is a very young girl. You must fuck a virgin. It costs a lot of money but it's worth it.'

'It's terrible,' said Marcellin to me, in English. 'That's what these people really believe. There are girls here—eight, nine, ten years old—and they have syphilis and gonorrhoea and they are wounded down there, too. These are not educated men.'

After supper I went to my tent to get my head-torch and was amazed to discover that the canvas roof of the tent had turned white: thousands of small translucent moths were crowding over it, their eyes glowing red in the torch beam like tiny cigarette-ends. As I watched, looking to see what they were doing—feeding? mating? migrating?—and wondering why you'd want to be white and visible at night if you were a moth, and why I was so ignorant about everything, Manou, in his silent way, appeared at my elbow.

'I have something important to tell you,' he whispered. 'Let's sit by the water. No one must hear us.'

'What is it?' I said with excessive eagerness.

'Last night, there was a snake,' he said quietly. 'Right beside us. Just where Nzé and I were sleeping.'

'But what was it?'

'We don't know. It was asleep under the leaves. Doubla and Vicky were making so much noise that we couldn't question it. You can only ask its name at night, in the silence.'

'So what happened?'

'We felt it after that, later on, right under the tarpaulins you gave us. It kept moving in the dark.' He straightened his shoulders and arched his spine. 'Nzé prayed to his grandfather. But his grandfather said he couldn't help us.'

'A burrowing python! That's what it was! They live underground in the Congo forest.'

'Whatever it was, real or not, it was sent to warn us.'

'Warn us?'

'Not to come here. Not to come to this place. And have you seen the waves?'

'Waves?'

'They come from the centre of the lake. Everyone has noticed. Marcellin saw it. There's something at the centre of the lake which lifts the water from below. Those waves, my friend, they have nothing to do with the wind.'

I was silent.

'Nzé and I—we are frightened. It's a great honour to be here, Redmon. No one in my family except Marcellin has ever been to this holy place. I will tell my children that I went to Lac Télé, and they will tell their children and their children's children. But this is enough. We must leave tomorrow.'

'I had a dream,' I lied, pleased with myself, feeling that I was getting the hang of things. 'We saw Mokele-mbembe and he made our fortunes.'

Manou stood up. 'You must be serious with me,' he said, disgusted. 'You can fool Marcellin, my friend, but not me. I can see the spirits in your face.' And he walked sharply back towards the fire.

I crawled into my tent, tied the flap securely, took off my boots, torch and glasses, lay down and wrapped myself in a tarpaulin. There were no roots or burrowing pythons beneath me; the ground squelched as I turned over; for the first time in months it was as soft as a mattress. The talk from the fire reached me as a murmur, the lake lapped gently at its bank and from among the chorus of frogs I picked out a note that was new to me: a double call like the bark of a vixen on a November night in Wiltshire. Someone began to snore, but with a resonance of such depth and volume that not even the giant of Boha could have produced it. It's Mokele-mbembe, I thought, and he must be hung with testicles as big as beer-barrels—when the reverberation signed itself off with a deep hoot, followed by three more, shorter and higher, and I realized it was just a pair of Pel's fishing owls (huge and brown with great round heads), hidden in the canopy somewhere nearby, agreeing that it was time to stop their marital cuddling on a high branch (they mate for life and sleep together), proclaim their territory, and go fishing (they watch for ripples on the surface in shallow water). As the male called again (he is said to be audible for a mile and a half) I wondered if I would live long enough to hear a Congo bay owl, which is known from only one specimen collected in 1951, told myself it was statistically improbable, blew a fuse in my brain and fell asleep.

In the half-light just before dawn, after a breakfast of boiled duiker bits and rice, Marcellin, Doubla and I bailed out the fishing canoe with our mess tins. A thick mist hung over the lake, unmoving.

'So where did you see the dinosaur?' I said.

Marcellin paused, as if I had been impolite. 'Over there,' he said, pointing off to the left. 'Three hundred yards out. But who knows? Perhaps it was a manifestation . . . ' His voice trailed off.

He looked intently at the now emptied bottom of the dug-out as if the pattern of adze marks in the wood might hold some meaning. 'And anyway,' he said, 'I'm not coming with you. *I hate this place.* I don't feel well. I've had enough. I have malaria. I'm going to stay in my tent. I'm going to stay in my tent all day long.'

He lowered himself to the ground like an old man, dropped his mess-tin in the mud, crawled into his tent and closed the flap behind him.

Doubla winked at me, touched the side of his nose with his forefinger and smiled broadly. His teeth, I noticed, were all in place. If anyone gets punched in the mouth round here, I thought, it isn't Doubla.

'Our Chief is a powerful man,' he said, shaking his head with admiration. 'He is making Marcellin suffer. He'll take his revenge —you watch. Marcellin sent our Chief to prison at Epéna. Our Chief is now sending Marcellin to prison in his own tent. And the prison at Epéna is much bigger and cooler than Marcellin's tent. Our Chief oversees everything that happens at this lake. This is our lake. It belongs to us, the *paysans*.'

I collected my hat, binoculars and water-bottle belt from my bergen, and joined Doubla and Vicky at the jetty. Nzé and Manou came to watch.

Doubla pulled two long-handled paddles from their hiding place in a bush at the edge of the promontory, laid his spear down the right-hand side of the dug-out, and climbed in after it with such ease and agility that I followed at once, without thinking: the narrow little craft yawed badly at the slightest uneducated movement; or, in other words, it suffered an attack of classical hysteria the moment I touched it, hurling itself left to right and back again, dementedly trying to fling me into the lake. 'Sit down!' yelled Doubla.

I managed to perch my buttocks on a log, my knees up to my ears.

'But I want to paddle!'

'Paddle! You don't know your arse from your tit!'

When the canoe calmed down enough for me to concentrate on a wider horizon, I became aware that Nzé, braying with laughter, had snapped to attention and was saluting. Manou however, having had no idea that such incompetence was possible, merely smiled, bemused. He looked concerned; I was touched. 'Keep still!' he shouted, as we pushed off. 'You fall over all the time! There's something wrong with your legs!'

No sound came from Marcellin's tent. He's slit his throat in there, I thought, as the promontory fell behind us in the mist.

As the sun rose, the mist grew whiter, thinned, dispersed and evaporated; three tsetse flies arrived over the canoe, buzzed Doubla's legs in a series of fast zig-zags and landed in the open spaces between the clumps of hairs on his right calf. Brown, with big heads and about half-an-inch long, they folded their wings like the blades of scissors and bit him. His leg twitched; he detached a hand from his paddle as it swung past, and, without interrupting his rhythm, slapped at them, hard, killing two. Inspecting my own legs I counted six on my trousers—I was anaesthetized from the waist down by my position on the log, I realized; I couldn't feel their probosces piercing my skin. In an hour or two I'd start to swell. It was extraordinary, I thought, that an insect with a reproduction rate slower than that of a rabbit could be Africa's most successful conservationist: it has been the sleeping-sickness-trypanosome-carrying tsetse fly (with a little help from the malaria mosquito and the Congo rapids) that has preserved this vast jungle for so long. If there had been none of the terrible fevers, the population of the Congo might be a great deal more than two million, and if it weren't for nagana, the sleeping sickness that kills cattle, both the Bantu and the white colonials might have begun to clear the forest in earnest.

And yes, I said to myself, momentarily glad I couldn't feel their bites, in the long term you have a lot to thank these flies for. But, a little voice said, you'll change your view of things, won't you, if you actually get the disease? And then, come to that, how do you know you haven't caught it already? After all, the symptoms listed in Elaine Jong's *The Travel and Tropical Medicine Manual* fit you rather well, don't they? The western form of trypanosomiasis, endemic here in the forest, starts with a tender papula within five to ten days of the tsetse bite and then ulcerates and disappears over two or three weeks (*and you've had plenty of those*). Next come intermittent fever, headaches and

Redmond O'Hanlon

tachycardia (*often*); then a transient skin rash (*not so transient round here*). Which is superseded by increasing indifference, somnolence and a reversal of the sleep cycle (*somnolent for years*). Which is in turn succeeded by incoordination, rigidity and Parkinsonian effect (*every night in Oxford, when drinking with the poet Craig Raine*), followed by irritability and periods of mania (*ditto, but then he always starts it*), stupor and indifference (*most mornings*) and finally death (*any minute now*).

Treatment is possible, if you can be bothered to get to a hospital, but then would you really want it when you get there? Suramin is fine, except that it's not particularly effective and produces proteinuria, fever and shock. So maybe Melarsoprol is better, because it's just a friendly little arsenic compound which at least penetrates the central nervous system and may leave you with nothing worse than optic atrophy and acute encephalitis. But, all in all, I suggest that perhaps you go for Pentamidine, because that will simply give you abdominal cramps, a sterile abscess and a spontaneous abortion.

'Quiet!' hissed Doubla, as I began to clap at my legs.

He crouched low, slid his paddle to the floor and reached for his spear. A brown hump, like the roundel of a shield, lay on the flat surface of the lake ahead. In one unbroken movement Doubla rose to his full height, leaned back slightly and, pitching forward, threw the spear with a force which would have been impressive even if his feet had been planted on the ground.

Two small waves collided where the turtle had just been, and spread out in concentric ripples. The shaft of the spear, sticking out of the water a yard off-centre, vibrated slightly. About seven feet of it was visible. So, I thought: let's assume that the point of the spear is buried one foot deep in the mud; that makes the lake, 100 yards out from the shore, around four feet deep. So maybe there are deeper pools in the middle. Or perhaps Mokele-mbembe is a very small dinosaur. Or maybe he is just a very flat dinosaur.

Doubla ran the canoe into a clump of arrow-plants, lopped a big green seed-pod from its stalk, cut it in half, cleaned out its seeds and handed one to me. 'You bail with them,' he said, pushing off again, keeping the canoe close in to the shore and rounding every little promontory.

Scooping out the water slopping round my ankles, I disturbed a tiger bittern in a reed-bed beside me. He rose into the air, a rustle of dark brown and reds like autumn leaves, and banked into the forest, his long yellow legs dangling behind him.

The tiger bittern, I thought, is very rare indeed (the great James P. Chapin only saw two on all his travels up the Congo river and explorations to the east) and if you heard its call for the first time, a deep single or double boom repeated for several minutes at dusk or in the middle of the night, a fog-horn of a note, it would be much more reasonable to think of monsters than of a shy brown bird. But then Doubla and Vicky, being local fishermen, would have heard it all the time. I'll show them its picture in Serle and Morel, I told myself pedantically, and see if they can imitate its call.

I counted five fish eagles at various points in the air above us, and I decided that I was almost happy, that I would forget about my numb bum and lost legs and the tsetse flies that I couldn't swat when, rounding the tangle of a fallen tree, Doubla saw something. He shot the canoe in under a clump of arrow-plants and we crept ashore.

Nothing moved; and then there was the sound of breaking vegetation in a patch of wild ginger. 'Look! Look!' yelled Doubla, pointing into the branches above us. 'It's one of his wives! The husband—he runs away! But look! One of his wives!'

The female gorilla sat in a high fork of the tree, plainly visible, and, through the binoculars, I looked straight into her shiny black face—at her averted eyes beneath the big protruding brow, her squat nose, the two linked horseshoes of her nostrils, her wide thin lips. She seemed extraordinarily human. I was seized with an absurd desire to hold her hand.

She appeared unsure what to do; she stood up, one hand grasping the branch above her, and sat down again. She was carrying something; there were two small black arms tight around her chest; she was carrying an infant.

'We need a gun,' said Doubla in my ear. 'Poof!'

'She's got a child,' I said, lowering my binoculars, afraid they might be a threat signal, an enlarged stare. 'We must leave her alone.'

'They're good to eat,' said Doubla, gesturing with his spear, 'they make you strong.'

'You shouldn't eat them,' I said, over-emotional, taking his arm, pulling him back towards the canoe. 'They're protected.'

'Protected! You white men. The ideas you have! Don't you eat gorillas in England? I bet you do. You're rich. Your forests must be *full* of gorillas.'

'There are no gorillas in England or anywhere else. They live only here and to the east. You should protect them.'

'Huh!' said Doubla, twisting his tendon-hard arm out of my grasp.

A big sitatunga, a swamp antelope, kicked up arcs of water as it made for the bank and safety. Eight long-tailed cormorants straggled past us and disappeared into the haze, a dancing migraine of heat. It was hot, sweaty, skin-crackling, painful.

We landed beside a raffia palm and walked a few yards through the bushes into a small clearing. A tree had been felled. 'This place belongs to my ancestors,' said Doubla. 'They come here to go fishing.'

He ran a hand across his stubbled chin and short moustache, pulled at his scraggy sideboards, reset his eyes and mouth into a mask even more implacable than his usual expression. He then shouted, listened, replied, listened, shook his head enigmatically and sat down on a log.

I took my water-bottle out of its belt-pouch and passed it to him.

'Look,' I said finally, feeling like some nineteenth-century ethnographer, 'I'm sure you can tell me the truth in this holy place. There's something I'd really like to know—have you seen Mokele-mbembe?'

'What a stupid question,' said Doubla, looking genuinely surprised. 'Mokele-mbembe is not an animal like a gorilla or a python. And Mokele-mbembe is not a sacred animal. It doesn't appear to people. It is an animal of mystery. It exists because we imagine it. But to see it—never. You don't see it.'

Half an hour later we put in to the bank beside two crossed

sticks driven into the mud. 'Crocodile eggs,' Doubla said. 'She will have finished laying by now.'

We struggled up a narrow flattened trail to a pile of leaves and twigs and loose soil about a yard high and six feet across. But something had got there before us. The nest-mound was open and fragments of brittle white shell lay scattered everywhere. Judging by the bigger pieces, the eggs must have been around three inches long and oval, perhaps those of the African slender-snouted crocodile. Doubla dug down with his hands. Nothing.

'The *zoko*'s had our supper,' he said.

'What's that? A marsh mongoose?' I said, excited. Or better still: perhaps the eggs were eaten by that long-nosed mongoose. ('Up to now only thirty specimens known . . . lives entirely in rain forests. No details of habits.')

Doubla shook his head.

'A servaline genet?' (Cat-sized, low-slung, black spots on ochre, long bushy black-ringed tail—'HABITAT: dense woodlands and primeval forests. HABITS: details not known.')

Doubla inflated his chest and cheeks like a bullfrog.

'A Congo clawless otter?' ('HABITS: little known.')

He put his right arm behind his buttocks and lashed it from side to side; he opened his mouth, displayed his thirty-two teeth and came at me with his fingers crooked rigid like claws. At this point I realized that he was trying to tell me something.

'Mokele-mbembe?'

'Much worse than Mokele-mbembe,' said Doubla with one of his short dry laughs, like the first warning bark of a dog that intends to take your leg off. 'The *zoko* is a real monster. He's bigger and faster than a man. And if you annoy him he attacks.'

He held his arms bent inwards at the elbow-joint and imitated something heavy trundling across the forest floor. He flicked out his tongue.

'A monitor lizard!' I yelled to myself. 'It's a Nile monitor!' (Six feet long, first appearing in the fossil record 130 million years ago: and having the good sense to lay its own eggs somewhere safe—by digging a hole in the side of a self-sealing termite's nest.)

A faint hooting call reached us: *woow-ooow-woow*.

Doubla hissed like a monitor: 'Chimpanzees!'

We followed the intermittent calls into a creek; an inlet sheltered from the lake, secluded and still, its surface covered in water-lilies.

We floundered ashore in silence; the bursts of chimpanzee conversation increasing in volume and coming from straight ahead. I scooped up handfuls of black mud and plastered my shirt and face with it.

We crossed two swampy streams, crawled on all fours across a patch of firmer ground and slithered on our stomachs to the base of a tree where an old male sat, half-way up on a big bough, slowly pulling twigs towards his surprisingly mobile lips, fastidiously biting selected leaves. Munching, he was deep in thought. He was almost bald, with big ears, deep-set brown eyes and a black face. Doubla put a finger in each nostril and made a high-pitched nasal grunting, the love-call of the male duiker. The old chimpanzee stopped munching, bent forward to look down, swung his head from side to side to get a view through the branches, saw us and took a huge piss. He put his elbow against the tree-trunk and ran a hand over his bald head and face and thought a bit, looking away.

'Waaaa!' he said.

Other chimpanzees immediately began to appear around us, all of them, as far as I could see from my position in the mud, with black ears, faces and palms and black skin on the soles of their feet—adult tschegos, I thought reassuringly, giving them a name. They're the western lowland rain forest variety in which only the very young have faces like white men.

They swung lower, crowding down towards us, until one was about thirty feet away and another above us. Two more, I noticed, were behind us.

The old male stood up on his bough, opened his mouth wide—transforming his peaceful face into a shocking display of Dracula canines—and screamed short, fast, ear-drum-cracking screams. He stamped on the bough and slapped the trunk of the tree. He gripped a small branch in each hand and shook them with appalling purpose.

The others joined in, their throat sacs distended with air and

76

indignation, their hair erect with rage. They whooped together, a *whoo-whooo-whooo* which increased in volume, a frenzy of screaming and branch-shaking. The male above us let fly an explosion of small round turds on our heads, a shotgun-blast of shit. It was unnerving to be the object of such concentrated dislike; no wonder even socially insensitive leopards turned and ran.

This is a very effective display, I thought, patronizingly. Then I thought (less patronizingly), these apes are big. And then I remembered Jane Goodall's account of the chimpanzee's idea of maximum excitement, a really good day out: you grab a young baboon or colobus by the foot, bash its brains out on a tree, rip it to bits and eat it. I had a sudden twinge of fear, and in the maelstrom of whirling sound-waves it was not amenable to reason. There was a stamping on the ground behind us. Doubla, obviously sharing my thoughts, jumped to his feet, shouted and banged the flat of his machete-blade as hard as he could against the tree-trunk.

The chimpanzees dropped to the ground and fled.

We reached camp well after dark. Nzé and Manou and the brothers came to greet us but Marcellin remained sitting in silence by the fire.

'Did you hear it?' whispered Manou, taking me by the arm the moment I stepped ashore, staring into my face, as anxious as I had ever seen him.

'Hear what? What's the matter?'

'It called this afternoon. We all heard it.' He made a thin, high-pitched cry, *ooo-ooo-oooo*. 'Nzé is frightened, too. Maybe things will not go well with us. Maybe we will not live to buy our bicycles with the money you will give us. If you hear Mokele-mbembe—you die.'

'It's the chimpanzees!' I shouted like a Bantu, feeling I had made a great discovery, my one contribution to science to date. 'It's the sound of chimpanzees! You're just not used to sound carrying across open spaces! You can't be. This is the biggest stretch of open water for hundreds of miles!'

'We heard Mokele-mbembe,' said Manou, completely unaffected by my logic. 'We're going to die.'

A fter supper, the Southern Cross bright above the lake, Doubla and I happened to be alone together, washing our mess-tins by the dug-out.

'So, Doubla,' I said softly, 'why did Marcellin swear he saw the dinosaur?'

'Don't you know?' said Doubla, giving me his first real smile, 'it's to bring idiots like you here. And make a lot of money.'

Pel's fishing owl began to call.

APRIL TALKS

The Backlash Against Feminism
with Susan Faludi, Susie Orbach and Marilyn French Thursday 2 April 19.30

The Creatures Time Forgot
On photography and disability imagery, with David Hevey and Eamonn McCabe
Tuesday 14 April 19.30

Andreas Serrano
Date to be announced

Russell Hoban
Thursday 23 April 13.00

Marge Piercy
Friday 24 April 13.00

Screen Censorship and Sexuality
Conference Saturday 25 April 10.00-18.00

Sattareh Farman Farmaian
Tuesday 28 April 13.00

Mark Cousins on Psychoanalysis and Space
Thursday 30 April 20.00

ICATALKS   Institute of Contemporary Arts, The Mall, London SW!
Box office 071 930 3647

ABRAHAM VERGHESE
SOUNDINGS

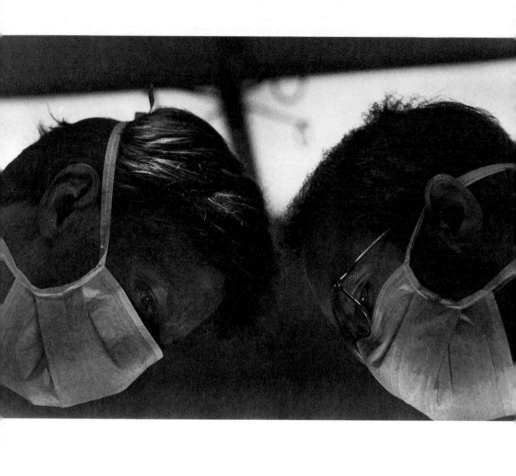

O n the first day of June, 1972, I was taught how to percuss the body. That night, lying flat on my back, the sheets pulled away and the lights off, I started just above my right lung, high, at the level of my nipple, pressing the middle finger of my left hand against my skin. I cocked my right wrist and let the fingertips fall like piano hammers: *thoom, thoom.*

'Resonance!' I said to myself, picturing the air vibrating in a million air sacs, a million tiny tambours.

I moved down an inch: *thoom, thoom.* Further down and further still, and then suddenly, *thunk! thunk!*—dullness. I had reached my liver, airless and solid.

I returned to my nipple: *thoom, thoom, thoom, thoom,* and then *thunk!* I lightened my stroke: there was no longer any sound but there was still a vibration in my stationary finger—the pleximeter finger—which told me where the air sacs ended and where, high under my rib cage, under the domed diaphragm, my liver began.

I traversed my liver, following its dull note into the belly until the *thunk! thunk!* was replaced by a sharp and high pitched *tup! tup!*—'Timpani!' It was the air that had been trapped in the loops of my bowel. No longer confined to little sacs, it was free to vibrate like the air in a conga drum—*tup! tup!*

I percussed everything. I percussed table tops, to find the stony dull circle where the leg joined the underside. I percussed plaster walls, looking for studs. I percussed tins of rice flour and the sides of filing cabinets. But in the dark it was my own body that I percussed. As I drifted to sleep I saw myself as if transparent, my viscera, both hollow and solid, shining through my skin.

T he man who taught me percussion was Charles Leithead, Professor of Medicine at the Princess Tsahai Hospital in Addis Ababa, Ethiopia. I was a third-year medical student. It was only two years before Haile Selassie was deposed and the country came unglued.

Professor Leithead, who favoured dark, pin-striped suits and Edinburgh ties, was bald except for a fringe of grey-white hair that hung long over his collar. Half-moon, tortoise-shell glasses

Photo: Eugene Richards (Magnum)

83

were perched on the very tip of his nose.

At the time that I came under his preceptorship, I harboured secret fantasies of specializing in heroic neuro-surgery, high-risk perinatology, surgery-of-the-open-heart-and-transplant kind—as did my two fellow students, Tom and Arsalon. We were convinced that it was only by specializing in these fields that we would achieve the Dr Kildare-ish charisma that we all secretly sought. As it turned out, most of us who met Leithead found a higher calling than surgery or perinatology: we became internists.

We met Leithead in the hospital every other afternoon for a bedside tutorial.

Leithead was about six foot two but had a way of slumping his shoulders and bending his knees when first introduced to a patient, as though trying to make himself more human. After introductions, he would sit by the bed and hunch forward, crossing his legs English style, and then—as if that had not been enough—would hook one foot behind the calf of the other leg so that he was now double-twisted, vine-like: a seated caduceus. The spectacles would come off and he would bend over as if studying the tile pattern on the floor. The Professor's command of Amharic was good enough, we suspected, for him to understand most of what transpired, but we translated for him nevertheless. The corners of his mouth would twitch, or his chin draw up as though he were going to cry as we gravely described the case before us.

One case I remember was that of Woizero Almaz. Arsalon described how her symptoms unfolded. Almaz, having squatted beside the market road to pee, noticed that her water was taking a dangerous course. Emerging from the perimeter of her skirts, the narrow groundstream had crept towards a nearby coil of rusty, evil-looking barbed wire. Since her water had touched the wire, Almaz had suffered pain in her hips, night-sweats, fever. Arsalon asked more questions, but Woizero Almaz looked only at the bald pate while answering. Her gaze remained rooted on the Great White One. When Arsalon finished his history, we all looked at each other while our preceptor continued gazing at the floor. Finally he spoke.

'Ask Woizero Almaz for me, would you, if . . . '—and the

questions, in a strange Yorkshire accent, would then emanate from this twisted vine, each one piercing some protected enclave that the patient—her eyes bugging out—had not thought fit to share with us. Now, terrified at the clairvoyance of this foreigner with the white mane and the black serpent of a stethoscope coiled in his hand, she spewed out reams of history, well beyond the tales of barbed wire and bad humours and evil miasma that we had heard thus far. Other patients had been known to throw in cries for forgiveness.

Leithead rose to examine the patient, bringing his head close to inspect her skin and her bony landmarks, then stepping to the foot of the bed and squatting to 'sight' down her body to see if both sides of the chest rose and fell equally. Only then did he begin probing with his fingers. He percussed smoothly, rhythmically and rapidly: quick strokes—*thoom-oom-oom*—before moving on, each triplet melodic and crisp, mapping out the borders of the lung, the edges of viscera, a silhouette of the heart. Finally, almost as an afterthought, he used his stethoscope. All this was done with great economy of time and motion, as if this was not an examination but some sort of bloodless surgery. Now, having understood the case, he demonstrated his findings to us, letting us see and feel and hear what he had experienced, leading us in Socratic fashion to a diagnosis. 'Never forget,' he would say: 'inspection, *then* palpation, *then* percussion, finally auscultation.' He would look at us curiously and ask: 'Which is the least important instrument in our armamentarium?'

'The stethoscope, sir!' we would bark out.

'And why is that, pray?'

'Because, sir,' we would chant, 'by the time you have looked, felt and percussed, you should know what you will hear!'

Twenty years later, medical students, interns and residents are waiting to make rounds with me. I am working in an intensive care unit in an American hospital, but percussion has lost none of its fascination for me. I have a recurrent fantasy involving percussion and Technicolor crayons. In it I work not on a patient but on an indulgent lover: I use my soundings to find her pituitary and mark it with a blue tear-drop on the centre of her forehead. Wavy green lines over her cheeks and eyelids outline her sinuses. I cover her breasts with a scarlet heart, giant red and blue vessels bursting from it. On her belly I reveal a purple spleen and a nutmeg liver, hovering, canopy-like, over her uterus, her fallopian tubes and her ovaries. Then she takes the crayons from me, percusses my body, draws on me. Then, and only then, do we bring our bodies together.

In the intensive care unit the Chief Resident is discussing the readings taken from a Swan-Ganz catheter that sits inside the heart of a Mr Tobias. This simple device is inserted into a vein in the neck and is then fed in until it reaches the right side of the heart, where all venous blood must go. This is done blindly at the bedside, no X-rays, just a green monitor that displays what the pressure transducer at the tip of the catheter conveys. Like an observer afloat inside the body, the transducer first shows the undulations of the venous waves, then the more defined swells of the atrium, the heart's receiving chamber.

Suddenly the monitor shows giant excursions, flicking up and down the screen; we are now in the heart's muscular pumping chamber: the ventricle. A small balloon at the tip of the catheter is inflated, and is carried into the circulation, riding like a barrel over a waterfall, into the pulmonary artery and out into the periphery of the lung, where it will remain, taking soundings and sending them back to the cockpit-like display over the patient's head.

These are still the days of 'aggressive' medicine in America. The Swan-Ganz catheter and the Intensive Care Unit are emblems of this aggression; to place a catheter into a neck vein is, for many a young intern, a mark of valour. As much as I am against this 'aggression' (are those of us who are less aggressive in some way negligent?), I cannot help being sympathetic, remembering my own post-graduate training on arriving in America. It was a time—just before AIDS—of unreal and unparalleled confidence, bordering on conceit. There seemed to be little that medicine could not do: while I, as a lowly intern, was inserting Swan-Ganz catheters, the cardiologists were using even more sophisticated catheters, inserting them in the leg and up into the aorta, then using tiny balloons and lasers to open clogged coronary arteries. These were the frontier days of the every-other-night call. We were the vaqueros of the fluorescent corridors, riding the high of sleep deprivation, dressed day or night in surgical scrubs, banks of beepers on our belts, our tongues quick with the buzz words that reduced patients to syndromes—'rule out MI,' 'impending DTs,' 'multi-organ failure'—with floppy tourniquets threaded through the buttonholes of our coats, our pockets cluttered with pen-lights, EKG calipers, stethoscopes, plastic shuffle cards with algorithms and recipes on them, hemostats like multi-purpose wrenches that found uses from roach clips to ear-wax dislodgers, seven-gauge, seven-inch needles with a twelve-inch trail of tubing carried casually in its sterile packaging, ready—should we be first at a cardiac arrest (a CODE BLUE)—to slide needle under collar-bone and into the great subclavian vein, feeding the serpent tubing down the vena cava in a cathartic ritual that established our mastery over the human body. There seemed no reason to believe, when AIDS arrived, that we would not transfix it with our divining needles, lyse it with our potions, swallow it and digest it in the great vats of eighties technology.

I examine Mr Tobias. Mr Tobias is ninety years old, has had a massive heart attack—his fourth—and is unlikely to make it out of the intensive care unit. The students and interns are wrapped up in the medical issues of his heart attack, in the urgency of a situation that has lost all its urgency for me. The debate goes from a pacemaker to digitalis. While they debate, I picture Sir William Withering, the discoverer of digitalis, holding foxgloves in his hand and wondering if they really cured dropsy, as his patients claimed. Secretly, I believe it was the word, *foxglove*. Listen to it: *fox* and *glove*. What incongruous images: how impossible not to smile. I would like to think that it was the sight of those long tubular flowers spilling from his fingers, purplish and vibrant, that made him pursue his investigations.

My mind drifts to Titian's *Venus of Urbino* which I saw last month in Florence. Maybe such a vision is what Mr Tobias needs—not digitalis—to restore to him a willingness to separate his mind from his diseased heart, to disconnect his rapid breathing from the anxiety that over the years has left deep wrinkles on his wrinkles. He needs to look at the smooth contoured flesh of the abdomen of Venus and cast away his Pall Mall cigarettes and his bacon-fat treats for ever. Not because they *will* kill him—he is ninety years old—but because thus far they have not. Instead they give him angina, repeated admissions to the ICU as small pieces of his heart die. I wonder, has Mr Tobias ever seen *Venus of Urbino*? I wish I carried a print in my black bag.

Would that I had the courage to prescribe:

Titian's *V.of.U.*
Sig: to be viewed every hour while awake.
NO SUBSTITUTION

Or better still, tape the picture to the ceiling above his bed.

My uncle carried a large black bag—five times as big as mine—which unfolded magically to reveal three tiers of shining ampoules: a mini-dispensary with digitalis, morphine, theophylline, ergot, adrenalin, stramonium, terramycin and many varieties of pills in the recesses below. Sometimes I went with him on his calls. He was a naturally muscled man, more suited to work in an iron foundry than to medicine, but there was also a delicacy in the way he felt the pulse, or placed his thumbs under the eyes and pulled down to reveal perfect red half moons peeking out at the world, or studied the tongue to divine in its markings—typhoid, malaria or dyspepsia. Once, a hysterical child came calling: his mother was down, 'looking like death.' My uncle and I went quickly—an urgent call! My uncle, after finding the pulse and listening to the heart through layers of traditional dress, injected Coramine. *Coramine*: those three syllables still evoke for me a dramatic rescue, the means to jump start a heart. The woman stirred. She sat up and rubbed her eyes, and then, seeing us, covered her face modestly with the end of her waist cloth. I put away the syringe in my uncle's bag, folded the shelves back inside, clicked it shut and proudly carried it for him. But I kept the empty ampoule of Coramine.

There are many distinct smells in medicine: the mousy, ammoniacal odour of liver failure—an odour always linked to yellow eyes and a swollen belly; the urine-like odour of renal failure; the faecal odour of a lung abscess; the fruity odour of a diabetic coma. As we enter the next room we encounter a smell that is not yet in the textbooks. It is the smell of the unremittent fever in AIDS, the one that goes on for months and months: it is the scent of a hot body; of skin that has lost its lustre and that flakes at the touch; of hair that has turned translucent and become sparse and that no longer hides the scalp. The scent is subtle but definitive, sweet, almost musky, like the smell of a sealed childhood room: a little stale, but filled with echoes of playful voices, giggles, music.

Tony, a young man, looks much worse than he did yesterday. His mother and father are in the room, pressed into one corner by our entry.

Tony's lips are cracked and his mouth is filled with white patches. He inhales air noisily and erratically into his windpipe, dispensing with the niceties of nostrils, lips or cheeks because of his air hunger. Wisely, many weeks ago, he vetoed a ventilator. A wavy frost line has formed over his forehead. Like the remnants left by waves on a beach, the salt from his sweat has condensed on his brow. His skin is hot to the touch.

I call out loudly: 'Tony!'

There is a perceptible raising of his eyebrows, a turn of his head, but the eyelids remain half-set. Underneath the lids, the eyeballs are roving, as if scanning the ceiling, searching for someone. This is 'coma vigil'. In the pre-antibiotic era, when nothing could be done for most fevers, physicians would painstakingly describe the 'typhoid state' as the terminal event. Tony has not only the 'coma vigil' of the typhoid state, but also 'muttering delirium' and 'floccillation'—picking at the bedclothes.

Tony's pulse is difficult to detect, a faint thread under my finger. His belly is scooped out and hollow. I can feel the edge of the liver, and on the left side the spleen which is much enlarged. As I press down on his flanks, I feel his kidneys slip under my palm with each breath he takes, pushed down by the descent of his diaphragm. The medical students and residents are quiet, hovering around the bed, uncomfortable because death is staring at them. I am uncomfortable too, but thankful to have the ritual of the examination. I palpate Tony's neck, armpits and groin for lymph nodes. I flash my pen-light into his pupils, nose, mouth. I pull out my stethoscope and listen over his neck, heart, chest, belly and femoral arteries. I unsheath my tendon hammer and tap his biceps, then his triceps. I move down to elicit the knee and ankle jerk. Then I flip the hammer over and use its pointed end to scratch softly at the soles of his feet, noting the brisk flexion of his toes and the extension of his big toe.

I have saved percussion for last.

I percuss his chest, and the sound of his right lung is disturbing. Only at the very top, near his collar-bone, do I hear the *thoom* of resonance. Below that, from above his nipple to his belly, it is dull; the sound is indistinguishable from the *thunk* of the liver. The lung has been transformed from a spongy, light, pliant organ to a solidifying, consolidating mass. The sounds of my percussion on his body fill the room. *Thoom, thunk, thunk, thunk, tup, tup, tup.* I glance at his parents. They listen to the sound of their son as if mesmerized. Once more: *thoom, thunk, thunk, tup, tup*—even Tony seems to pause in his delirious muttering, his floccillation, to listen to the music, to relax, to smile.

My tools—the hammer, the flashlight, the stethoscope—are scattered on his bed. As I pick them up one by one, I realize that all I had to offer Tony was the ritual of the examination, this dance of a Western shaman. Now the dance is over, and the beeps and blips of monitors register again, as does the bored voice of an operator on the overhead speaker summoning someone *stat.*

We exit the room and in the chilly hallway our small group is subdued. We have six more patients in the intensive care unit to see. We move on resolutely, wheeling the silver chart rack in front of us. My heart is heavy. I am already thinking of nightfall, of the comfort of my bed, my body.

MICHAEL DIBDIN
THE PATHOLOGY LESSON

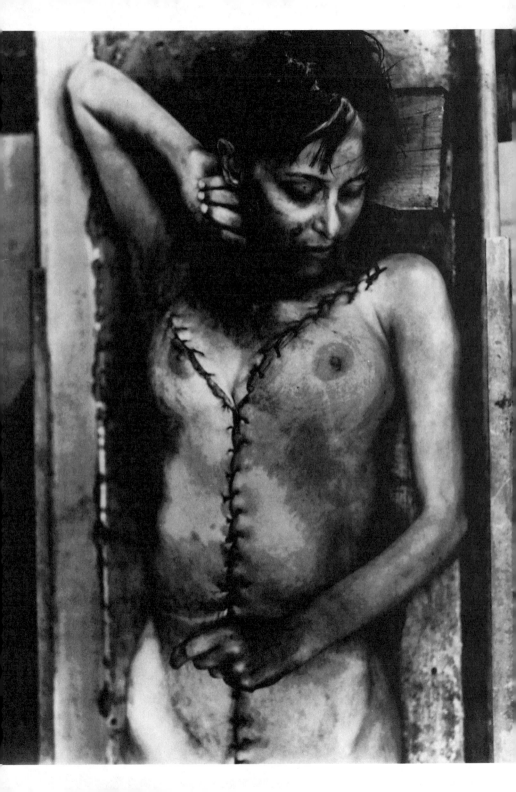

The subject is wheeled in on a trolley, swathed in white linen, an amorphous bundle whose only distinguishing features are the peak of the feet at one end and a red stain at the other. The assistant manoeuvres the trolley alongside one of the six stainless-steel tables, their surfaces covered in an elaborate system of grooves and canals, each ending in a drain. He puts on a pair of disposable plastic gloves and starts to unwrap the sheeting. The corpse is female, in her late forties. The red stain is due to a flow of gore from the mouth, which has dribbled over the lips and chin like food sicked up by a drunk.

The assistant slides his hands under the thighs and upper back and flips the corpse over on to the waist-high table. It bounces slightly, like a plank. A brown luggage label bearing the woman's name and dates of birth and death dangles from the big toe of her left foot. The toes are cramped and pinched from a lifetime in tight shoes. The left arm is bent up at the elbow, the hand raised as though waving. The assistant grasps the wrist and bears down, arm-wrestling with the dead. A sound like knuckles being cracked signals his victory over the rigor mortis, and he lays the now-docile limb down on the table.

Apart from some long dark marks near the throat, the skin of the upper body is a very pale off-white, the tone of beeswax or old ivory. By contrast, the lower half is covered in huge livid blotches, as though heavily bruised. This condition, known as post-mortem hypostasis, is caused by the uncirculated blood draining downwards under its own weight and saturating the vessels. The body retains a pair of white panties whose presence in this context is as embarrassing as their absence would be in the world we left behind at the door. The pathologist's assistant—a mild, shy man whose Gloucestershire burr is occasionally disturbed by a stutter—removes them with a pair of scissors.

From a rack by the wall he selects a wooden block about six inches thick. A semicircular notch in one side supports the neck of the corpse in the manner of a travel pillow, holding the head steady with the face upturned. With a small-bladed scalpel, the assistant sets about making a straight cut across the top of the scalp from one ear to the other. This is not easy, as the long hair keeps fouling the blade and handle. When the incision is complete, the assistant runs the knife along under the cut edge on both sides, working the two halves of the scalp free of the skull. He then grips the front flap and, with surprising ease, pulls it down like a stocking mask over the woman's face. The revealed surface of subcutaneous fat is sheer glistening yellow, mottled by the tiny blood-vessels of the dermis. Where it ends, just above the mouth, bushy tufts of hair protrude like the false moustache of an operatic bandit. The assistant lays a piece of linen torn from an old sheet over the head, to help him get a grip. Then he takes a small rectangular woodsaw in the other hand and gets to work on the skull.

It is a typical Monday morning in the post-mortem room of a large regional hospital. According to the plan displayed in the entrance hall, the windowless ground floor of the main building contains the emergency department, operating theatres and intensive care wards. This leaves about a third of the floor area unaccounted for, a blank on the chart. In the corridors, signs leading to this *terra incognita* are discreetly marked 'Histopathology'. Once inside, indications of what goes on here become slightly more explicit. A closed door bears a handwritten notice: CUT-UP IN PROGRESS—DO NOT ENTER. 'This sink not to be used for dissections as waste disposal unit is broken,' warns another. On the laboratory benches, slivers of flesh marinate in jars of pinkish liquid, each with a label identifying the body— dead or alive—from which it was removed. The air reeks with the heady odour of formaldehyde.

The laboratory is still deserted. Medical students supposedly choose pathology because it is a nine to five job—the dead are undemanding patients—but the doctor I am with prefers to make an early start. Post-mortem examinations represent a minor and not particularly interesting part of his work, which centres on diseases of the lung and kidney. Most of his time is divided between analysing the results of biopsies and his teaching duties at the local university, but he is also obliged to do his share of the PMs required by local coroners, which usually total about fifteen a week. He prefers to get this chore out of the way before the laboratory staff arrive.

It is now ten past eight. While the assistant prepares the female cadaver at the next table, the pathologist is occupied with the first of the two cases for examination this morning, an elderly man who died five days earlier after complaining of abdominal pain. Even to an untrained eye, this comes as no surprise. Repeated surgery for cancer of the intestines has created a dense, matted web of ugly scar tissue, while a recurrence of the cancer has led to the secretion of huge amounts of an acrid yellow liquid that has flooded the entire abdominal cavity, mingling with the creamy slime oozing from the intestine itself to form a murky soup out of which coils of gut surface like the tentacles of an octopus.

The pathologist battles gamely on, struggling to grip the slippery tissue so that he can hack it free with a scalpel, pausing from time to time to bail out with a large kitchen sponge. Somewhere nearby a telephone starts ringing. It sounds exotically normal. The pathologist's assistant puts down his saw, wipes his rubber gloves on the blood-stained rag and pads off to answer it. The post-mortem room is a quiet place: the muffled footfall of calf-length rubber boots, the swish of the white plastic aprons, the click and tinkle of metal instruments, the drumming of liquid draining into the steel pans under each table. After muttering in an undertone for some time, the assistant returns with a message for the pathologist, who is still up to his wrists in the man's bowels. 'No, I can't see him tomorrow,' he says. 'Ask him if he's free for lunch on Thursday.' Having relayed this response, the assistant returns to his corpse and picks up the saw again.

When the intestines have finally been sorted out and removed, the pathologist moves on to the other abdominal organs. In the living body, fluttering like a bird in the costal cage, the heart may be the centre of attention, but once stilled it is a shapeless, unremarkable mass of tissue. The undisputed stars of the post-mortem are the liver and brain. The latter has already been removed and weighed, and is resting on the marble slab at the end of the dissection table, where it is now joined by the liver. They make an apt pair, weighing in at about a kilo and a half each, much the same size but a complete contrast in appearance. The brain is all delicate filigree, intricate folds and convolutions

95

of a curd-like oyster-white material that, despite its bulk, looks as insubstantial as whipped egg-white. If this is Mind, the liver is all Body: a massive glistening lump the consistency and colour of freshly-ploughed clay.

At least, *this* one is, but it may not be typical. As the pathologist has just remarked with a sigh, 'In a case like this, it's not so much a question of finding the cause of death as marvelling at the fact that he was still alive.' The man's abdominal cavity is a disaster area, his liver is cirrhotic, the lung tissue a mosaic of black soot particles and the kidneys severely damaged. Any of these things could—and with time, would—have resulted in death, yet in fact none of them did. Sectioning the heart in thin slices, the pathologist discovers an accretion of yellow, gristly material in the coronary artery. Only a few millimetres of the vital vessel are occluded, but it was enough to pre-empt all the other diseases and disorders that had been queuing up to kill the man. The pathologist notes his findings and takes samples and cuttings for analysis. The first of the two post-mortems is complete.

Except in its adverbial form, 'post-mortem' is a virtual neologism, dating back no further than the early Victorian era. Before that the word used was 'autopsy', which, like much early English lexis, is still current in the United States. Rather surprisingly, the original sense of the term—*auto-opsis*—has nothing to do with death, or indeed with medicine. It means simply 'seeing for oneself', personal observation. In the Roman era the bodies of murder victims were commonly displayed so that the public could personally satisfy themselves of the fact and manner of the crime. Early English law required coroners and juries to view the bodies of those who had died in suspicious circumstances, but it was not until the late nineteenth century that modern techniques of forensic examination on scientific principles became widely established. 'Autopsy' continued to retain its popular appeal, however. As late as the mid-1860s, Zola could write:

The morgue is a show within reach of every purse, to

which passers-by both rich and poor can freely treat themselves. The door stands open, anyone can walk in. Some enthusiasts go out of their way so as not to miss a single one of these productions. When the slabs are bare, people leave feeling frustrated, swindled, muttering under their breath. When the slabs are well-stocked, and there is a fine display of human flesh, the visitors jostle each other, indulge in a little easy emotion, scare themselves silly, crack jokes and clap or boo, just like at the theatre. Then they leave, well-satisfied, remarking that the Morgue really went well this time.

In this regard, the last hundred years have seen a more profound shift in practice and opinion than the preceding thousand. At the age of forty-four, I had never seen a corpse until this morning, and I am both astonished and reassured to see just how dead they look. As a child at the theatre, I was always disappointed to see the corpse get up and take a curtain call along with the rest of the cast. There is clearly no risk of such improprieties here. Both the man and the woman look as though they've been dead for years rather than days. They look as if they've been dead for ever, as if they were *born* dead. Throughout their ordeal, both corpses radiate a total passivity, a massive indifference, like stuffed toys whose mutilated features and unstitched seams need cause no anguish. Nothing that matters can happen to the dead, and nothing that happens to them can matter.

Which is just as well, given what *is* happening. We have moved over to the other table by now. The pathologist explains that the woman had been discovered lying face down in her back garden at twenty to eleven the previous morning, and suicide is suspected. About an hour and a half before the woman's daughter and son-in-law discovered the body, she had apparently chatted briefly over the garden fence to her neighbour. The latter said that she had seemed in good spirits, but the coroner's letter noted a history of depression for which the woman had been taking various drugs. An overdose of one of these seems the most likely cause of death. The livid marks around the neck area probably indicate that the victim made a preliminary attempt to cut her throat.

The first step is to expose and remove the brain. The assistant fits a circular clamp around the woman's skull and tightens a long metal screw resting on the forehead. The differential of pressure creates a fault along the line of least resistance, in this case the circular groove he has just sawed around the upper cranium. With a dull crack, like a stubborn walnut, the skull cap pops loose. The organ itself drops out as easily as a VW's motor. The pathologist slices through the four connecting arteries and then severs the lower part of the brain-stem, a thick cluster of nerve fibres that in section resembles a heavy-duty two-ply power cable. Cradled like a baby in the pathologist's palms, the brain looks too large to fit into the container from which it has just emerged. The explanation comes when you look inside the emptied skull and realize that the cranial cavity extends all the way down the back of the head to a point level with the mouth. There's nothing there now but a small puddle of rich thick blood covered in a haze of fine white bone-meal that has dropped off the caul enclosing the brain itself.

Turning his attention to the body, the pathologist proceeds just as he had earlier with the man, making an incision from a point just below the Adam's apple to one just above the navel, then bifurcating towards each hip. The short blade slips easily through the bloodless flesh, as unresistant as putty. In the belly area, a subcutaneous layer of honey-coloured fat appears. The woman's abdomen could hardly present a more complete contrast with that of the cancer sufferer we have just examined. Each organ is clean, whole, well-formed and separate. The pathologist hauls out yards of chitterlings as easily as a conjuror producing the flags of all nations from his hat. He slits open the *boudin blanc* of the stomach and takes a sample of the grey slime inside for later analysis, before drawing off urine from the bladder and blood from the carotid artery. The advent of North Sea gas, he explains, has made his job a lot more difficult. In the old days, most suicides stuck their heads in the oven, and since coal gas has the effect of turning every internal organ of the body bright pink, diagnosis was a doddle. Now the preferred method is poison, the discovery of which can take up to fifty laboratory-hours. 'Twenty years ago it was nearly always an overdose of barbiturates. Then they clamped down on prescribing them, so now people use all sorts of weird and wonderful mixtures.'

Now it is the turn of the thoracic cavity. Working with rapid slits of the scalpel, the pathologist cuts through the dark chest meat and peels back the vest of flesh to reveal the rib-cage. This is less of a barrier than it appears, thanks to the soft costal cartilage joining the ribs to the breastbone. The pathologist slices through this and removes the sternum. The Argument from Design has been long discredited, but its seductive attractions are evident when you look inside the human body. Everything seems so lovingly packaged and arranged, like a cabin trunk stowed against breakage with just those items necessary for the voyage. And in the present case, they seem to have survived intact. The liver looks in perfect condition, the lungs are as pink as a baby's. At the next table meanwhile, the pathologist's assistant is reassembling the other cadaver with slightly less than exquisite care. The sawn cap of bone is replaced on the skull and a bandage coated with plaster of Paris wound around the suture. While it dries, the assistant closes up the body cavity with big coarse stitches, like a seaman mending sail. Lacking the resilience of living tissue, the back and buttocks look flattened and wrinkled, like a face pressed against a pane of glass.

All that remains in the female cadaver is the apparatus of the respiratory system, which has to be removed *en bloc*. This involves freeing the trachea, larynx, oesophagus, pharynx and tongue, and it is hard work. At the bottom of the faceless face, the mouth opens and the lips quiver like those of a sleeper disturbed by bad dreams. The spasm subsides as the pathologist lifts the last of the pink tubing clear of the body. In the voided chest cavity, the ridge of the spine rises to separate two dark tarns of blood. The pathologist slits the throat open to make sure there is no obstruction that might have caused choking. The tongue, a grey naked lump of flesh, dangles like a flaccid penis.

All the organs have now been weighed and placed on the marble slab for individual dissection. The fundamental principle of modern forensic pathology is that every cavity and every important organ of the body must be examined, even when the cause of death seems obvious. In the present case, although suicide by poisoning remains the most likely hypothesis, other causes of sudden death such as a brain haemorrhage must also be considered. As we proceed, however, the growing weight of negative evidence seems to preclude the possibility of natural death. Each organ turns out to be a textbook example of health and vigour. 'That's what kidneys should look like!' the pathologist exclaims enthusiastically, splitting them like oysters to reveal the pink cortex and the fan-like fibres of the medulla. The heart, too, its workings laid bare by the long-bladed pathology knife, proves to be in prime condition. 'We've got people queuing up for valves like these.' He holds the brain in his left hand and slices it into thick slabs that tumble over slowly. The cut surface has the dull sheen of polished marble. There is not a speck of blood to be seen. The pathologist sighs. A kindly man, he knows the suffering that a suicide can cause a family. But the negative evidence of the post-mortem is overwhelming. 'She was good for another forty years,' he remarks as he strips off the rubber gloves and washes his hands.

The autopsy is complete. I thank the pathologist, who thanks me for coming. We both thank the assistant, who in turn thanks us. It is all very polite, very English. You almost expect the cadavers to add their thanks as well. At home, I put all my clothes through the wash and take several showers, but the volatile formaldehyde vapours seem to have penetrated my flesh and I smell like a corpse myself for several days. Memories of the post-mortem prove even harder to dispel, in particular the contrast between the two deaths.

The man was murdered by his heart, his life choked off as surely as by the hands of a strangler. The organ we had taken from the woman's body could have saved him, although he would have needed her lungs, liver and all the rest as well. Nevertheless, there was no mystery here, no sting. His death made sense. He was a perfect subject for the post-mortem, obeying its laws and resigned to its judgements.

The woman, on the other hand, escaped us. Her body was

'good for another forty years', but it hadn't stood a chance. First she went for it with a knife and then, when it survived that, finished it off with poison. The pathologist could determine no more than the proximate cause of death: an overdose of anti-depressants. The final cause remained unknown, despite the radical deconstruction we had carried out. When so much had been laid bare, this remaining shred of mystery seemed more intolerable than ever. Presumably there must have been some fault that we couldn't quite trace, some sclerosis of love or gradual haemorrhage of meaning that eventually proved fatal. But the exact pathology of this condition, its nature, cause and treatment, eluded us.

The author would like to thank Doctor Michael Dunnill, Fellow of Merton College, Oxford, for his invaluable collaboration.

Always the woman's languor, the same folds
in the sheets, the same dark corners of the room,
always the lamplight strikes her breasts and
cheekbones at the same angle, and always the silk
shawl and the dark hair falls with the same
delicacy.

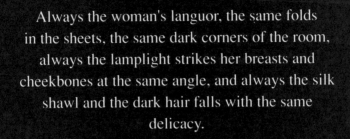

The Stories of
Eva Luna

ISABEL
ALLENDE

In Penguin
£5.99

MARY ELLEN MARK
SPRING BREAK
AT DAYTONA BEACH

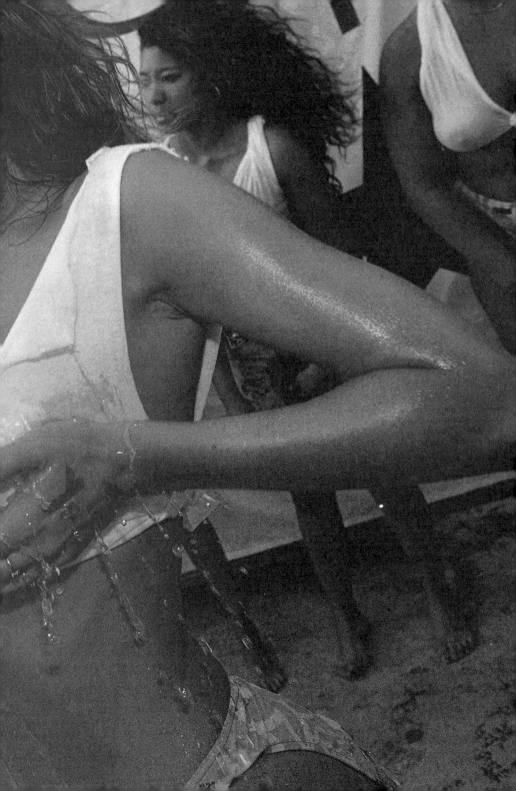

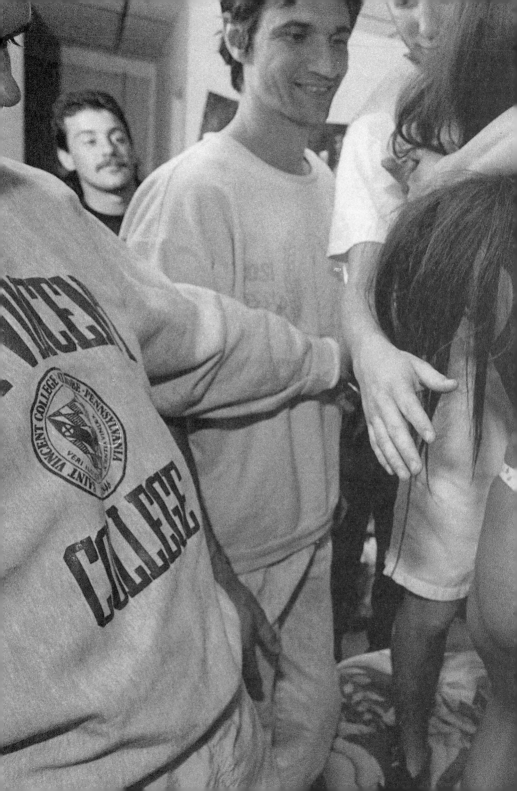

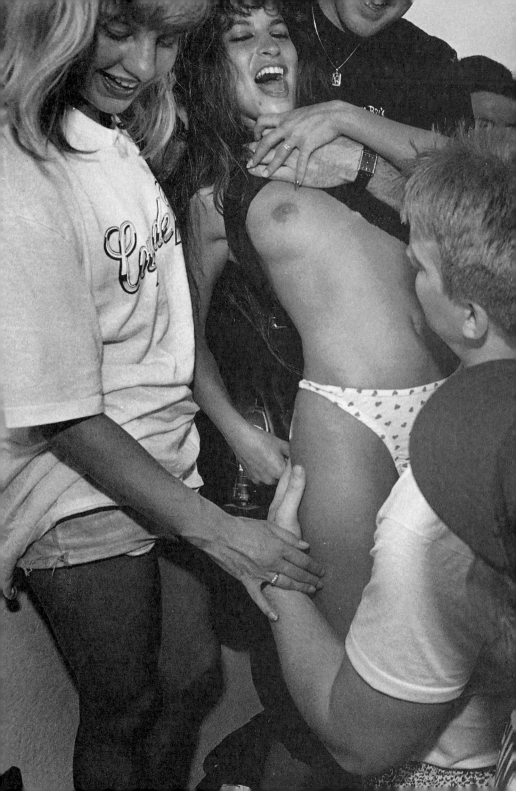

JEANETTE WINTERSON
THE CELLS, TISSUES,
SYSTEMS AND CAVITIES
OF THE BODY

In bereavement books they tell you to sleep with a pillow pulled down beside you. Not quite a Dutch wife, that is a bolster held between the legs in the tropics to soak up the sweat, not quite a Dutch wife. 'The pillow will comfort you in the long unbroken hours. If you sleep you will unconsciously benefit from its presence. If you wake the bed will seem less large and lonely.' Who writes these books? Do they really think, those quiet concerned counsellors, that two feet of linen-bound stuffing will assuage a broken heart? I don't want a pillow, I want your moving breathing flesh. I want you to hold my hand in the dark, I want to roll on to you and push myself into you. When I turn in the night the bed is continent-broad. There is endless white space where you won't be. I travel it inch by inch but you're not there. It's not a game, you're not going to leap out and surprise me. The bed is empty. I'm in it but the bed is empty.

The next day I cycled to the library but instead of going to the Russian section as I had intended I went to the medical books. I became obsessed with anatomy. If I could not put Louise out of my mind I would drown myself in her. Within the clinical language, through the dispassionate view of the sucking, sweating, greedy, defecating self, I found a love-poem to Louise. I would go on knowing her, more intimately than the skin, hair and voice that I craved. I would have her plasma, her spleen, her synovial fluid. I would recognize her even when her body had long since fallen away.

The multiplication of cells by mitosis occurs throughout the life of the individual. It occurs at a more rapid rate until growth is complete. Thereafter new cells are formed to replace those which have died. Nerve cells are a notable exception. When they die they are not replaced.

In the secret places of her thymus gland Louise is making too much of herself. Her faithful biology depends on regulation but the white T-cells have turned bandit. They don't obey the rules. They are swarming into the bloodstream, overturning the quiet order of spleen and intestine. In the lymph nodes they are swelling with pride. It used to be their job to keep her body safe from enemies on the outside. They were her immunity, her certainty against infection. Now they are the enemies on the inside. The security forces have rebelled. Louise is the victim of a *coup*.

Will you let me crawl inside you, stand guard over you, trap them as they come at you? Why can't I dam their blind tide that filthies your blood? Why are there no lock-gates on the portal vein? The inside of your body is innocent, nothing has taught it fear. Your artery canals trust their cargo, they don't check the shipments in the blood. You are full to overflowing but the keeper is asleep and there's murder going on inside. Who comes here? Let me hold up my lantern. It's only the blood; red cells carrying oxygen to the heart, thrombocytes making sure of proper clotting. The white cells, B and T types, just a few of them as always whistling as they go.

The faithful body has made a mistake. This is no time to stamp the passports and look at the sky. Coming up behind are hundreds of them. Hundreds too many, armed to the teeth for a job that doesn't need doing. Not needed? With all that weaponry? Here they come, hurtling through the bloodstream trying to pick a fight. There's no one to fight but you Louise. You're the foreign body now.

Tissues, such as the lining of the mouth, can be seen with the naked eye, but the millions of cells which make up the tissues are so small that they can only be seen with the aid of a microscope.

The naked eye. How many times have I enjoyed you with my lascivious naked eye. I have seen you unclothed, bent to wash, the curve of your back, the concurve of your belly. I have had you beneath me for examination, seen the scars between your thighs where you fell on barbed wire. You look as if an animal has clawed you, run its steel nails through your skin, leaving harsh marks of ownership.

My eyes are brown, they have fluttered across your body like

127

butterflies. I have flown the distance of your body from side to side of your ivory coast. I know the forests where I can rest and feed. I have mapped you with my naked eye and stored you out of sight. The millions of cells that make up your tissues are plotted on my retina. Night flying I know exactly where I am. Your body is my landing-strip.

The lining of your mouth I know through tongue and spit. Its ridges, valleys, the corrugated roof, the fortress of teeth. The glossy smoothness of the inside of your upper lip is interrupted by a rough swirl where you were hurt once. The tissues of the mouth and anus heal faster than any others but they leave signs for those who care to look. I care to look. There's a story trapped inside your mouth. A crashed car and a smashed windscreen. The only witness is the scar, jagged like a duelling scar where the skin still shows the stitches.

My naked eye counts your teeth, including the fillings. The incisors, canines, the molars and premolars. Thirty-two in all. Thirty-one in your case. After sex you tiger-tear your food, let your mouth run over with grease. Sometimes it's me you bite, leaving shallow wounds in my shoulders. Do you want to stripe me to match your own? I wear the wounds as a badge of honour. The moulds of your teeth are easy to see under my shirt but the L that tattoos me on the inside is not visible to the naked eye.

For descriptive purposes the human body is separated into cavities. The cranial cavity contains the brain. Its boundaries are formed by the bones of the skull.

Let me penetrate you. I am the archaeologist of tombs. I would devote my life to marking your passageways, the entrances and exits of that impressive mausoleum, your body. How tight and secret are the funnels and wells of youth and health. A wriggling finger can hardly detect the start of an antechamber, much less push through to the wide aqueous halls that hide womb, gut and brain.

In the old or ill, the nostrils flare, the eye sockets make deep pools of request. The mouth slackens, the teeth fall from their first line of defence. Even the ears enlarge like trumpets. The body is making way for worms.

As I embalm you in my memory, the first thing I shall do is to hook out your brain through your accommodating orifices. Now that I have lost you I cannot allow you to develop, you must be a photograph not a poem. You must be rid of life as I am rid of life. We shall sink together you and I, down, down into the dark void where once the vital organs were.

I have always admired your head. The strong front of your forehead and the long crown. Your skull is slightly bulbous at the back, giving way to a deep drop at the nape of the neck. I have abseiled your head without fear. I have held your head in my hands, taken it, soothed the resistance, and held back my desire to probe under the skin to the seat of you. In that hollow is where you exist. There the world is made and identified according to your omnivorous taxonomy. It's a strange combination of mortality and swank, the all-seeing, all-knowing brain, mistress of so much, capable of tricks and feats. Spoon-bending and higher mathematics. The hard-bounded space hides the vulnerable self.

I can't enter you in clothes that won't show the stains, my hands full of tools to record and analyse. If I come to you with a torch and a notebook, a medical diagram and a cloth to mop up the mess, I'll have you bagged neat and tidy. I'll store you in plastic like chicken livers. Womb, gut, brain, neatly labelled and returned. Is that how to know another human being?

I know how your hair tumbles from its chignon and washes your shoulders in light. I know the calcium of your cheek bones. I know the weapon of your jaw. I have held your head in my hands but I have never held you. Not you in your spaces, spirit, electrons of life.

'Explore me,' you said and I collected my ropes, flasks and maps, expecting to be back home soon. I dropped into the mass of you and I cannot find the way out. Sometimes I think I'm free, coughed up like Jonah from the whale, but then I turn a corner and recognize myself again. Myself in your skin, myself lodged in your bones, myself floating in the cavities that decorate every surgeon's wall. That is how I know you. You are what I know.

The Skin

The skin is composed of two main parts: the dermis and the epidermis.

Odd to think that the piece of you I know best is already dead. The cells on the surface of your skin are thin and flat without blood-vessels or nerve-endings. Dead cells, thickest on the palms of your hands and the soles of your feet. Your sepulchral body, offered to me in the past tense, protects your soft centre from the intrusions of the outside world. I am one such intrusion, stroking you with necrophiliac obsession, loving the shell laid out before me.

The dead you is constantly being rubbed away by the dead me. Your cells fall and flake away, fodder to dust mites and bed bugs. Your droppings support colonies of life that graze on skin and hair no longer wanted. You don't feel a thing. How could you? All your sensation comes from deeper down, the live places where the dermis is renewing itself, making another armadillo layer. You are a knight in shining armour.

Rescue me. Swing me up beside you, let me hold on to you, arms around your waist, head nodding against your back. Your smell soothes me to sleep, I can bury myself in the warm goosedown of your body. Your skin tastes salty and slightly citrus. When I run my tongue in a long wet line across your breasts I can feel the tiny hairs, the puckering of the aureole, the cone of your nipple. Your breasts are beehives pouring honey.

I am a creature who feeds at your hand. I would be the squire rendering excellent service. Rest now, let me unlace your boots, massage your feet where the skin is calloused and sore. There is nothing distasteful about you to me; not sweat nor grime, not disease and its dull markings. Put your foot in my lap and I will cut your nails and ease the tightness of a long day. It has been a long day for you to find me. You are bruised all over. Burst figs are the livid purple of your skin.

The leukaemic body hurts easily. I could not be rough with you now, making you cry out with pleasure close to pain. We've bruised each other, broken the capillaries shot with blood; tubes hair-thin intervening between arteries and veins, those ramified blood-vessels that write the body's longing. You used to flush with desire. That was when we were in control, our bodies conspirators in our pleasure.

My nerve-endings became sensitive to minute changes in your skin temperature. No longer the crude lever of Hot or Cold, I tried to find the second when your skin thickened. The beginning of passion, heat coming through, heart-beat deepening, quickening. I know your blood-vessels were swelling and your pores expanding. The physiological effects of lust are easy to read. Sometimes you sneezed four or five times like a cat. It's such an ordinary thing, happening millions of times a day all over the world. An ordinary miracle, your body changing under my hands. And yet, how to believe in the obvious surprise? Extraordinary, unlikely that you should want me.

I'm living on my memories like a cheap has-been. I've been sitting in this chair by the fire, my hand on the cat, talking aloud, fool-ramblings. There's a doctor's textbook fallen open on the floor. To me it's a book of spells. Skin, it says. Skin.

You were milk-white and fresh to drink. Will your skin discolour, its brightness blurring? Will your neck and spleen distend? Will the rigorous contours of your stomach swell under an infertile load? It may be so and the private drawing I keep of you will be a poor reproduction then. It may be so but if you are broken then so am I.

The Skeleton

THE CLAVICLE OR COLLAR-BONE: *the clavicle is a long bone which has a double curve. The shaft of the bone is roughened for the attachment of the muscles. The clavicle provides the only bony link between the upper extremity and the axial skeleton.*

I cannot think of the double curve lithe and flowing with movement as a bony ridge, I think of it as the musical instrument that bears the same root. Clavis. Key. Clavichord. The first stringed instrument with a keyboard. Your clavicle is both keyboard and key. If I push my fingers into the recesses behind the bone I find you like a soft-shell crab. I find the openings between the springs of muscle where I can press myself into the chords of your neck. The bone runs in perfect scale from sternum to scapula. It feels lathe-turned. Why should a bone be balletic?

You have a dress with a *décolletage* to emphasise your breasts. I suppose the cleavage is the proper focus but what I wanted to do was to fasten my index finger and thumb at the bolts of your collar-bone, push out, spreading the web of my hand until it caught against your throat. You asked me if I wanted to strangle you. No, I wanted to fit you, not just in the obvious ways but in so many indentations.

It was a game, fitting bone on bone. I thought difference was rated to be the largest part of sexual attraction but there are so many things about us that are the same.

Bone of my bone. Flesh of my flesh. To remember you it's my own body I touch. Thus she was, here and here. The physical memory blunders through the doors the mind has tried to seal. A skeleton key to Bluebeard's chamber. The bloody key that unlocks pain. Wisdom says forget, the body howls. The bolts of your collar-bone undo me. Thus she was, here and here.

THE SCAPULA OR SHOULDER-BLADE: *the scapula is a flat triangular shaped bone which lies on the posterior wall superficial to the ribs and separated from them by muscle.*

Shuttered like a fan no one suspects your shoulder-blades of wings. While you lay on your belly I kneaded the hard edges of your flight. You are a fallen angel but still as the angels are; body light as a dragonfly, great gold wings cut across the sun.

If I'm not careful you'll cut me. If I slip my hand too casually down the sharp side of your scapula I will lift away a bleeding palm. I know the stigmata of presumption. The wound that will not heal if I take you for granted.

Nail me to you. I will ride you like a nightmare. You are the winged horse Pegasus who would not be saddled. Strain under me. I want to see your muscle skein flex and stretch. Such innocent triangles holding hidden strength. Don't rear at me with unfolding power. I fear you in our bed when I put out my hand to touch you and feel the twin razors turned towards me. You sleep with your back towards me so that I will know the full extent of you. It is sufficient.

THE FACE: *there are thirteen bones that form the skeleton of the face. For completeness the frontal bone should be added.*

Of the visions that come to me waking and sleeping the most insistent is your face. Your face, mirror-smooth and mirror-clear. Your face under the moon, silvered with cool reflection, your face in its mystery, revealing me.

I cut out your face where it had caught in the ice on the pond, your face bigger than my body, your mouth filled with water. I held you against my chest on that snowy day, the outline of you jagged into my jacket. When I put my lips to your frozen cheek you burned me. The skin tore at the corner of my mouth, my mouth filled with blood. The closer I held you to me, the faster you melted away. I held you as Death will hold you. Death that slowly pulls down the skin's heavy curtain to expose the bony cage behind.

The skin loosens, yellows like limestone, like limestone worn by time, shows up the marbling of veins. The pale translucency hardens and grows cold. The bones themselves yellow into tusks.

Your face gores me. I am run through. Into the holes I pack splinters of hope but hope does not heal me. Should I pad my eyes with forgetfulness, eyes grown thin through looking? Frontal bone, palatine bones, nasal bones, lacrimal bones, cheek bones, maxilla, vomer, inferior conchae, mandible.

Those are my shields; those are my blankets; those words don't remind me of your face.

Jeanette Winterson

The Special Senses

HEARING AND THE EAR: *the auricle is the expanded portion which projects from the side of the head. It is composed of fibro–elastic cartilage covered with skin and fine hairs. It is deeply grooved and ridged. The prominent outer ridge is known as the helix. The lobule is the soft pliable part at the lower extremity.*

Sound waves travel at about 335 metres per second. That's about a fifth of a mile and Louise is perhaps two hundred miles away. If I shout now, she'll hear me in seventeen minutes or so. I have to leave a margin of error for the unexpected. She may be swimming under water.

I call Louise from the doorstep because I know she can't hear me. I keen in the fields to the moon. Animals in the zoo do the same, hoping that another of their kind will call back. The zoo at night is the saddest place. Behind the bars, at rest from vivisecting eyes, the animals cry out, species separated from one another, knowing instinctively the map of belonging. They would choose predator and prey against this outlandish safety. Their ears, more powerful than those of their keepers, pick up sounds of cars and last-hour take-aways. They hear all the human noises of distress. What they don't hear is the hum of the undergrowth or the crack of fire. The noises of kill. The river-roar booming against brief screams. They prick their ears till their ears are sharp points but the noises they seek are too far away.

I wish I could hear your voice again.

THE NOSE: *the sense of smell in human beings is generally less acute than in other animals.*

The smells of my lover's body are still strong in my nostrils. The yeast smell of her sex. The rich fermenting undertow of rising bread. My lover is a kitchen cooking partridge. I shall visit her gamey low-roofed den and feed from her. Three days without washing and she is well-hung and high. Her skirts reel back from her body, her scent is a hoop about her thighs.

From beyond the front door my nose is twitching, I can smell her coming down the hall towards me. She is a perfumier of sandalwood and hops. I want to uncork her. I want to push my head against the open wall of her loins. She is firm and ripe, a dark compound of sweet cattle straw and Madonna of the Incense. She is frankincense and myrrh, bitter cousin smells of death and faith.

When she bleeds the smells I know change colour. There is iron in her soul on those days. She smells like a gun.

My lover is cocked and ready to fire. She has the scent of her prey on her. She consumes me when she comes in thin white smoke smelling of saltpetre. Shot against her all I want are the last wreaths of her desire that carry from the base of her to what doctors like to call the olfactory nerves.

TASTE: *there are four fundamental sensations of taste—sweet, sour, bitter and salt.*

My lover is an olive tree whose roots grow by the sea. Her fruit is pungent and green. It is my joy to get at the stone of her. The little stone of her hard by the tongue. Her thick-fleshed, salt-veined swaddle stone.

Who eats an olive without first puncturing the swaddle? The waited moment when the teeth shoot a strong burst of clear juice that has in it the weight of the land, the vicissitudes of the weather, even the first name of the olive keeper.

The sun is in your mouth. The burst of an olive is breaking of a bright sky. The hot days when the rains come. Eat the day where the sand burned the soles of your feet before the thunderstorm brought up your skin in bubbles of rain.

Our private grove is heavy with fruit. I shall worm you to the stone, the rough swaddle stone.

THE EYE: *the eye is situated in the orbital cavity. It is almost spherical in shape and about one inch in diameter.*

Light travels at 186,000 miles per second. Light is reflected into

135

the eyes by whatever comes within the field of vision. I see colour when a wavelength of light is reflected by an object and all other wavelengths are absorbed. Every colour has a different wavelength; red light has the longest.

Is that why I seem to see it everywhere? I am living in a red bubble made up of Louise's hair. It's the sunset time of year but it's not the dropping disc of light that holds me in the shadows of the yard. It's the colour I crave, floodings of you running down the edges of the sky on to the brown earth on to the grey stone. On to me.

Sometimes I run into the sunset arms wide like a scarecrow, thinking I can jump off the side of the world into the fiery furnace and be burned up in you. I would like to wrap my body in the blazing streaks of bloodshot sky.

All other colours are absorbed. The dull tinges of the day never penetrate my blackened skull. I live in four blank walls like an anchorite. You were a brightly lit room and I shut the door. You were a coat of many colours wrestled into the dirt.

Do you see me in my blood-soaked world? Green-eyed girl, eyes wide apart like almonds, come in tongues of flame and restore my sight.

GEOFFREY BIDDLE
MY DAUGHTER

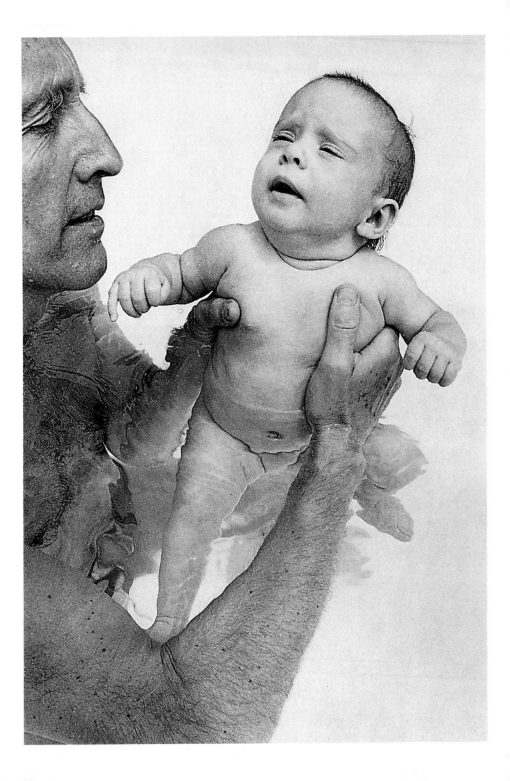

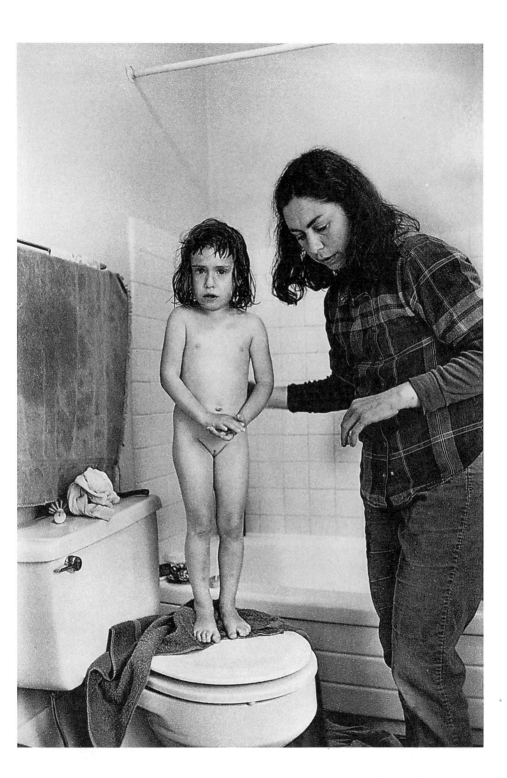

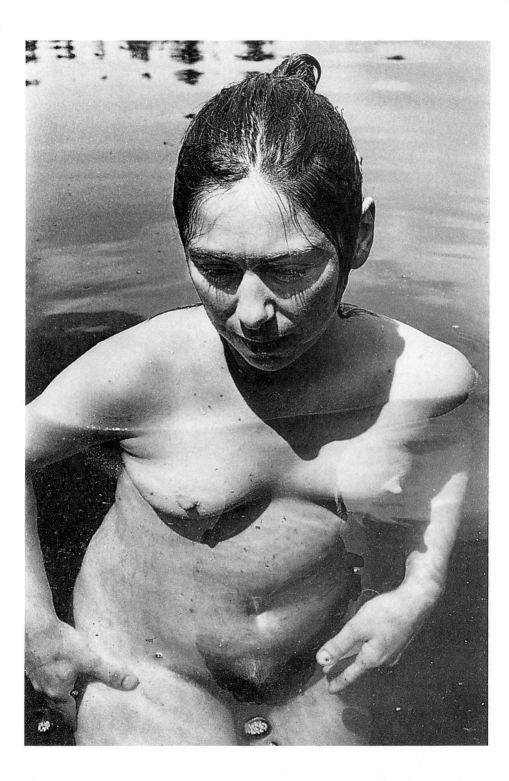

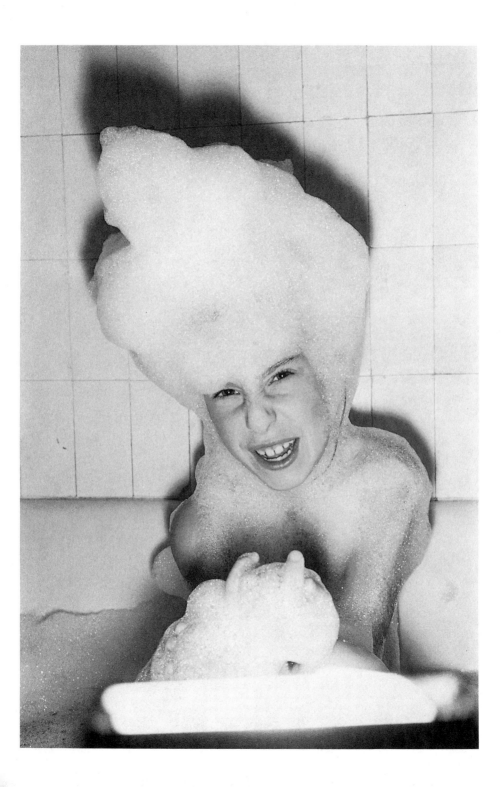

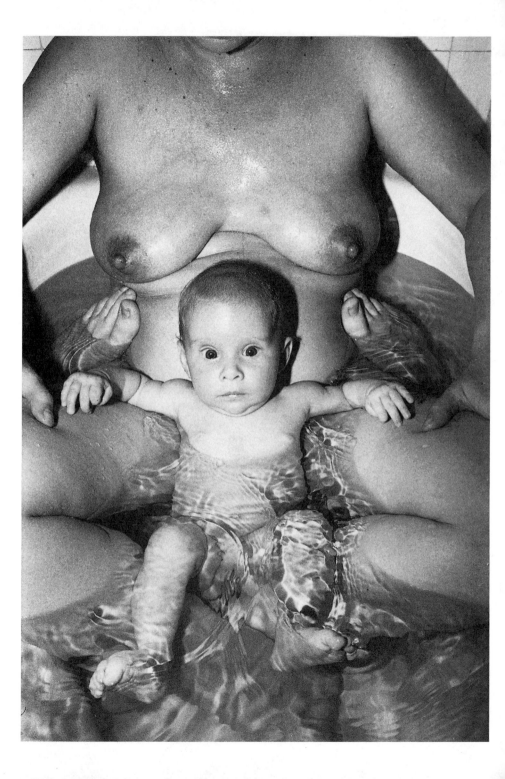

TODD MCEWEN
MY MOTHER'S EYES

My mother has a small brown book, the kind of notebook made of alligators and sold to wealthy people who do not make notes. In it she wrote down what a doctor told her on a bright day thirty years ago:

> You have a severe case of primary glaucoma. This is a disease the cause of which we don't know. I must tell you the utmost vigilance and sacrifice on your part are required if you want to retain your sight. As long as I have been in practice I have longed for the day when I would be sure I would never, ever have to tell someone this. But here I am again, having to tell you. I'll do everything I possibly can.

In the alligator notebook my mother described her doctor's hands, which trembled. The light of matches he kept trying to put to his pipe wavered in the dim office. To her they must have been bright, her pupils surprised with ephedrine. It was hot outside; the air conditioner sucked up the smoke of the doctor's pipe. His square glasses and his white smock combined to make him an archetype of medicine.

Did she buy the notebook on the way home?

Along the branches of the fifth nerve pain travelled. The only great pain or wound to our family. Towards us, through our mother.

Along the fifth nerve, radiating like the system of the freeways. On a sunny day in Southern California, where there was to be no disease. We lived in concrete, in plastic, in sugar. Newborn, on television. I had never seen a single living thing sicken, or die. You might scrape your knee; mercurochrome was the only medicine I knew.

Dad helped Mother from the car. Over the black driveway, hot in September.

Dad said, your mother is very sick.

They had induced a glaucoma attack in order to measure the tension in the eye. Her eye. She did look ill. She was white and could not walk.

I asked, *are* you sick?

It wasn't that I didn't want to believe Dad, but that I didn't want to believe my eyes.

Mother managed to say, yes.

They had put her in the dark, alone in the dark for an hour, and then made her drink a quart of water. An attack came, slow pain becoming blinding.

What did she think about? The only light from the projection chart and the waiting slit-lamp.

The problem is the illiterate, the less literate, the less intelligent patient. It's hard to impress them with the seriousness. It's an unrelenting job looking after this disease. The patient has to do it.

We are not WASPs, but we are reserved by nature. We are full of squashed turmoils which must be old. Economies of movement which speak volumes. Longtime American Scots and Dutch, generations of laconic Ohio English, Michigan *meshugass.*

Our avoidance of: everything. But not like Connecticut bankers and other scared-cats. More from Scottish fears of disgrace and of goblins.

Dad put me in the kitchen and told me the disease was aggravated by stress. We must be kind to your mother.

What stress? California was new and it roared. There were many things to buy. How to understand what adults are talking about?

She wanted to spare us. Disease to be stamped out by hiding it. By not mentioning it. The only way to get along in this lie of a land. Do like the others. Everything's great. New car? More wine?

For Mother the vacuity of the place must have been a source of real, tooth-grinding tension, sick-making the idleness and rudeness of our neighbours.

My mother's sensibilities. My mother was formed in books and their pictures. A house surrounded by trees as if from Ohio. Her emotions, deep ones, are built of printed words. Dickens, Charlotte Brontë and Rafael Sabatini taught her how to live when she was a girl.

157

Far into every night with a pot of coffee and a pack of Camels, her father read. This was what all the driving, selling, arranging, scrimping and arguing of adult life was for: to have time to read.

Our neighbours waved and barbecued and swam. Southern California was empty and ugly to my mother. They talked of nothing—the insularity concomitant with money-gathering had begun.

The streets became littered with barefoot children and with the wrappers of things. The gardener did not know what chives were and tore them out of the ground wherever he found them. To him, everything that was not dichondra or geranium was anathema. The gardener of a woman who thought, who lived by the rhythms of poets she had effortlessly breathed in.

She had never imagined that her children's playmates would swing cats around their heads or write on walls or shit in their own closets.

Glaucoma threatened the very *method* of my mother. The time might come when she could no longer read, when words might become aural, different things. Deprived of their look, their measure. If she went blind she would miss the pleasure of seeing tree, ocean, ramshackle, Sonoma. More than seeing trees or even being able to get around the house.

She would find herself at the mercy of Dad and the *Orange County Register*. Or bores. Or THE FIFTY THOUSAND WATT CLEAR-CHANNEL VOICE OF KFI LOS ANGELES!

Was it this prospect, more than pain, which made her weep in dark rooms? We knew she did that. Or was it the pain, which was profound?

It could not be controlled. To the hospital, up on the hill: iridectomy.

Seeing your parent bandaged. My distress over this replaced the persistent memory of her ill on the hot driveway. And there is something of nightmare in a binocular bandage. Bad movies, helplessness. War, poppies. It seemed for ever that she lay in bed. I hated the metal shield which peeked, a sieve, from her bandage. Hated the smell of cellophane tape. Hated the dinners from cans Dad made.

One evening I cried and begged for pancakes, the only thing he knew how to make from scratch.

So arrived some women in a series. To help us. Two were genuinely kind, and never have I treated people so badly. I snapped at the women, insulted their cooking and what I felt to be their filthy, intrusive habits.

When I entered the phase of puberty which revels in dead bodies and bats, I embarked on the hobby of theatrical make-up. I sat in front of a mirror for hours, deforming my face with wire, plastic loops, stinking mixtures of liquid latex, gauze and mortician's wax.

I read instructions for the *Quasimodo effect*, covering your eye with putty and installing a blind plastic one down the cheek.

The fat boy next door tormented me. He played on his phonograph a George Jessel record, 'My Mother's Eyes', and snickered. I tried to kill him by pushing the fence over on to him.

He had once sat on Dad's mandolin.

Everything somehow had to do with eyes. Eyes were all sick or bad or bound to be injured.

Boys from across the street imprisoned me in a box. I, Young Scientist of the Space Age, began calmly perforating an escape hatch, with a miniature screwdriver. One of the boys tried to see in at me and got poked in the eye. He screamed and ran off. I stayed in the box, worrying about eyes, all the eyes of the world, and felt like a killer. He returned after a couple of days with a black patch and from that time on he wore glasses.

My sister and I were playing in the yard, throwing the vegetation around. A birch cone exploded in her face. Her eye was filled with small papery dots. The ease of the weekend, another bright day darkened with the doom of emergency.

Meeting the doctor at his office—he in sports clothes, turning on the lights, readying the instruments himself, wondering where things were, like Dad in the kitchen.

And then to see my sister, tiny, hysterical rather with fear and the anger of adults than from pain, being held down on a metal table as the tall doctor moved over her with needles and an undine.

159

And then my eye: ptosis. I was taken to the hospital one day and fed on frozen 7-Up. The doctor tucked up my eyelid, neatly, so that it would never quite close. They bandaged both my eyes.

I was frightened to awake from the anaesthesia, sick and not able to see. I said something and vomited into the dark. A nurse said, oh, are you feeling sick?

A boy in the bed next to me had wholly burned himself with fireworks. He was older and joked crudely with the nurses. But he was very ill and eventually he vanished.

My mother came to visit me in the afternoons. She could still see to drive then. As she read to me I pushed up the corner of one of my bandages. I could see her hands, and I cried silently, and the bandage came loose. At night I lay in the hospital bed and thought about bandages and eyes. I wondered if my mother pushed up a corner of her bandages to see my father as he sat beside her.

We lived in the factory of the future, on the lip of the desert of the bombs. At the edge of space travel. Girls and boys played with miniature rockets and space helmets. Cowboys and GIs banished for ever. I had a microscope, books about mummies, a rock collection.

I wanted to be clinical and careful, reasonable, like Dad.

On Saturdays he took us to the library. I discovered a copy of *May's Diseases of the Eye*. It poised me on the edge of emotional outer space. I was taken aback and nauseated by the watercolour plates of all these sick eyes. And by the seemingly unavoidable cruelty of medical texts. *In occasional cases there will be progressive diminution of vision despite all operations . . . in absolute glaucoma, with repeated attacks of pain, enucleation is indicated.*

A photograph of a baby suffering congenital glaucoma due to birthmarks: the large dark eyes of my mother.

My fears grew that one day she would become Plate 20-A, Acute Congestive Glaucoma, her eye a frightening red and black Mars.

On the day I took up my first job, I recognized the baby's dark eyes and my mother's in my office partner, a courtly Cuban

NO
STAMP
REQUIRED

GRANTA
FREEPOST
2-3 Hanover Yard
Noel Road
London
N1 8BR

NO
STAMP
REQUIRED

GRANTA
FREEPOST
2-3 Hanover Yard
Noel Road
London
N1 8BR

professor. I watched him lean back in his chair with his eye dropper every few hours and immediately took him as a friend for ever because he was brave.

All the Californians driving, driving from doctor to doctor through the very air which makes them ill. The misery and fatigue of thousands of physicians who look at a person and see an enemy.

My mother was waiting to see her doctor. A woman with sick eyes sitting in the row of chairs was weeping. Her tests had been a complete failure. She kept repeating the words *blind, blindness.* While others looked on and thought about bandages and eyes, and the light streamed in the window like a reminding, nagging slit-lamp, my mother got up and went over to the woman. With resolve and firmness she held her shoulder and her hands. She comforted her.

THE
SPECTATOR
SUBSCRIBE TODAY!

RATES

	12 months	6 months
UK........................... £71.00		£35.00
Europe......Airmail...... £82.00		£41.00
USA..........Airspeed... US$110		US$55
Rest of......Airmail...... £98.00		£49.00
World.......Airspeed.... £82.00		£41.00

Students: £35.50 (12 months):........ £27.00 (6months)

I enclose my cheque for £———————— *(Equivalent $US & Eurocheques accepted)*

Please tick:VISA ☐   ACCESS ☐   AMEX ☐   DINERS ☐

Card No: ☐☐☐☐☐☐☐☐☐☐☐☐☐☐☐☐☐☐☐

Card Expiry Date: ——————————

Signature: ————————————— Date: ——————————

Name: ——————————————————————————

Address: ——————————————————————————

—————————————————————————————————

————————————————————— Postcode: ——————————

Please send to: The Spectator Subscription Dept, PO Box 14, Harold Hill, Romford, Essex RM3 8EQ
☐ *Please tick here if you do not wish to receive direct mail from other companies.*

GIORGIO PRESSBURGER
TEETH

Giorgio Pressburger

One day in January a tall thin man with long white hair came into our courtyard. He was draped in a green cloak, torn in various places. He turned his face up to our balcony, spread his arms and began to speak with a resonant voice. I was frightened, but Mother explained that the man, a beggar, was reciting something.

'Reciting?' I didn't know the word.

Mother explained what it meant, and I turned back to the beggar.

His speech concerned the various ages of man, from when he is mewling in the cradle, to when he becomes adult, combative and quarrelsome, and at the end grows weak again, trembling, powerless.

'Last scene of all, which ends this strange eventful history,' said the beggar, 'is second childishness, and mere oblivion, sans teeth, sans eyes, sans taste, sans everything.'

He removed his dentures for this last part, drawling the words and forcing the sibilants to accentuate his own decrepitude. When he said the words 'sans everything' he dropped his arms and sobbed in a distressing manner. It was no longer a performance; he was exposing his own terrible misery. We threw him a coin and so did some of the other occupants of the block. The beggar—an old out-of-work actor—dried his tears and silently collected the money that had landed on the yellow tiles of the courtyard. Then he went on his way with his eyes to the ground.

My mother was moved. 'The poor man,' she murmured, and returned inside to prepare dinner.

This man who had aged instantaneously when his cheeks had grown flabby (with his false teeth in his mouth he did not look nearly so ancient) has always remained in my memory. When I think of him I feel like a child of six, with every stage of my life still ahead of me. This trick of the mind has always involved my teeth. In fact, from the very day of the apparition of the old actor in our courtyard, my teeth became an obsession. My tongue began to examine them every morning after I got up, and to send news to my brain about every tiny scratch, every movement, everything new.

164

The first time I dreamt of losing my teeth I was about thirty years old. I had just been sacked by the State Import–Export Agency and had taken charge of a firm distributing Hungarian handicrafts. One night, exhausted—my son Aronne had been born three days earlier—I went to sleep on the sofa, fully clothed. In my dream I felt with my tongue that my upper left canine was moving, rocking back and forth just as my milk teeth had done when I was a child. I took the canine between index finger and thumb, and verified with astonishment that I was able to draw it easily from the gum. Then, just as I had drawn it out, I was able to put it back into place, and the canine cemented itself securely in the jaw. 'How strange!' I thought and, still disbelieving, tried the whole operation again. I met with the same result as before. I woke with a sense of anguish, because I retained the fear that one day the canine might come out of its socket and fall into my soup, or on to the pavement, or that I might swallow it with my morning coffee. But there had been pleasure in the dream too: the salty taste of the gum brought to mind the taste of my wife Rachele. Some months later, when Aronne had taken on the shape of a real human being, the dream came again and the anguish, tinged with pleasure, was renewed. I researched the possible psychological significance of this nocturnal vision, noting with a certain sense of superiority the differences of opinion that were held on this subject.

Twenty years later the dream became dramatically real.

I was in Milan together with a large number of Hungarian drums and bottles of spirits destined for the Italian market. After a heavy meal, I noticed, passing my tongue over the surface of my teeth, that the edge of the gum was raised, partly covering my lower molars. Brushing my teeth that evening, I was forced to note that a great deal of blood issued from my mouth. My gums were sore; their inflammation disturbed me.

'What can it be?' I asked the colleague travelling with me.

'As far as I know, your gums play up like this in cases of syphilis and also with certain forms of leukaemia. Let's hope it isn't that.'

'I'm done for,' I thought. I felt defenceless, marked, ashamed at my imminent death.

‘**I**s it true what my friend said?' I asked the doctor I went to see the next day.

Doctor Ernesto Weiss, a former *émigré* to Israel who had subsequently moved to Italy, lowered his voice. 'Why do you always think the worst? I know pessimism is part of our character—and probably a constructive attitude—but here you are dealing with a simple inflammation.'

'What kind of inflammation?' I asked, partly relieved, yet concerned by this new uncertainty.

'The name of the illness is periodontitis, and I have to tell you that in most cases it leads to the early and unavoidable loss of all teeth.'

'I'm going to lose the lot?'

'Yes, inevitably.'

'How long will it take?' I asked, between hope and desperation.

'Fifteen, twenty years.'

At this moment my love for my physical appearance suffered irreparable damage. 'It is better to die!' I thought, 'than to be reduced to a defenceless monster.' But then another idea struck me. 'It doesn't matter. When all my teeth have fallen out, I'll put in some decent dentures. Better than that, I'll cement false teeth in my gums. It is not so easy to reduce a man to one of the toothless grotesques Leonardo drew. We do not have to accept desolation. We have the weapon of intelligence!' Yes, I dared to challenge my destiny, even the naked facts of existence and suffering. I was repaid with a challenge.

Doctor Weiss described to me the nature of the illness: there was an hereditary component against which it was impossible to fight, but much depended on the attention that I gave to the care of my gums and teeth. 'You have neglected them, even though they are a part of that body which lives with you on this earth, at least for the time being.'

The responsibility was mine, therefore. His declaration revealed a sad truth. 'The mechanism in which we are enclosed is not perfect,' I thought. 'We must take constant care of it. What can be the sense in all this? It is not to death that we are condemned, but to the imperfection of our bodies. If even the capacity for resisting pain and illness is written into our organism, where lies our freedom of choice?'

Anyhow, in the following years I applied myself, ten minutes a day—five in the morning and five in the evening—to the care of my teeth. I learned to use a silk thread to get between the gaps; I took to using antiseptic mouthwashes, to pushing the toothbrush against the edge of the gums and making the bristles penetrate inside the purse between flesh and enamel. In spite of all this I eventually found my canine with its root uncovered and black. When I smiled at my son, he began to cry.

'Dirty!' he wailed, pointing at my jaw with his finger. 'Nasty!'

Rachele, taking advantage of my being fired by the Popular Handicraft Export Firm and therefore of the interruption of my constant travels, fixed an appointment for me with Doctor Grossman, who had opened a surgery in Via Aurora.

'You have terrible breath. You must do something.' Rachele whispered to me one night, laying her head on my chest.

I did not trust Doctor Grossman, fearing his geniality and his youth not less than his rough hands with their dry skin. When at the end of the visit he declared that the root of my canine was carious and needed filling, and that besides I required 'a general cleaning', I got scared and did not turn up for my next appointment. On my own initiative I began to make mouthwashes with Odol and nothing else. When I went to Hamburg for a two-year stint as a lecturer in the Institute of Finno-Ugric Language and Literature, I left my wife and my children—including my recently born son Gersone—with my father, the ritual butcher of the district. The 'general cleaning' and the filling of the carious root of the canine were done in Doctor Bernheim's clinic in Mowestrasse, in the centre of that city. The doctor given the task of demolishing the greeny-yellow deposits of tartar, the crystallized food-remnants between the teeth, was a young Romanian woman, addressed by her colleagues at the clinic as 'Doctor Angela'. She was very beautiful. Her short, red hair brought out the strong but regular features of her face. She had a light and harmonious way of walking; her hands moved my head with barely perceptible caresses. During the first session she began

167

to grapple with the tartar so energetically I shed tears. Through the tears I noted the intensity of her gaze. Her eyes were grey-blue, large and round, the eyebrows fine and arched. She fixed on my mouth a stare of the most intense concentration. 'She looks like this at filth, at the dregs of being. So how will she look at my soul?' I asked myself.

Doctor Angela showed no inclination to talk to me except about oral hygiene. 'Be patient,' she said every so often, poking, tugging, scraping my teeth.

I wept great irrepressible tears.

'Don't despair,' she said to me once. 'There are worse things in life: illness, hunger, thirst, old age.' She was hurting me; the pain was spreading through my head so that I could think of nothing but my suffering.

One day she stroked my cheek tenderly. 'Poor thing,' she said, 'I seem to have touched your tear-duct. How will you cry when you really have a reason? All through life we have to suffer great pain, but it would be terrible if it were not so.' She murmured this with such a resigned objectivity that I was compelled to wonder if she realized that she was literally torturing me. At the end of the session I explained this to her.

'Yes, yes,' she said, disbelieving. For Doctor Angela pain was the fabric of existence, the foundation of everything, the eternal music.

I was displeased that the course of treatment had to come to an end. 'I hope I'll see you again,' I said, getting rid of the tissue paper and the plastic bib that Doctor Angela had wrapped me up in. It was the last session; the May afternoon was quiet.

'Perhaps we will meet again,' she said. 'While you still have some teeth there will always be the chance, and I will always be here in Hamburg; my husband's job is here.' The subtle tone of regret that I thought I heard in her voice encouraged me to ask if I could see her that evening. She did not say no, but she did point out that Doctor Maurer, her husband, a businessman, would come too. The three of us met at a vast resort beside the lake. We drank tea and ate pastries.

'Look, I made you cry, I hurt you, but far more painful is the

loss of something still living: a limb, or the heart, or a tooth.'
Angela smiled with her beautiful lips, that evening painted a
vivacious pink.

'The doctor is wrong,' I thought. 'The pain of absence
diminishes after a while. Man can get used to everything.' To be
frank, I have never known whether one should consider this
characteristic a good thing or the major defect of humanity, but I
know that parting that evening from Doctor Angela filled me
suddenly with a painful sense of deprivation.

We subsequently had a long, a very long correspondence that
ended only after I lost my last molar. I learned from her letters
that during the war Angela had lost all her relations; they had
died under jets of poison gas from showers in an extermination
camp. For decades the faces and voices of her parents and her
elder brothers returned in her dreams as if time hadn't passed.
The pain of this loss was a counterbalance to the love for me that
Angela expressed in her letters—she had gone as far as describing
to me the odour of her body and had asked me to do the same.
But the torment of loss was the sole true pleasure of her life: for
me, naturally, it was just a torment. Now that I wear a cheap set
of dentures, I think often of my teeth—and of Angela—and, like
her, tell my story for a particular reason: I hope to mitigate the
suffering caused by loss, a deep suffering, similar to that brought
on by the thought of death.

I must finish talking about my first upper left canine. After the
'general cleaning', Doctor Bernheim himself, the clinic's
proprietor, filled the cavity. I refused an injection and
confronted the drilling without a moan. I came out unharmed
from the operation, though the intensity of pain had made me
think I was close to death. My canine was now incredibly white
and smooth. But, with the passage of time, the tooth began to get
longer and longer. Every time I stopped in front of a mirror, I
raised the upper lip with my finger and looked at the state of my
canine. I did not dare to look at it for more than a few seconds,
though this was long enough to see the unstoppable retreat of the
gums, until one day it seemed that my upper left canine—with all
its horsy length—could fall out at any moment. Towards my sixty-

fifth year the tooth began to move a little, and then my dream of so long ago suddenly returned. One morning the canine came out without any pain. But it was impossible to reattach it, and to that extent my dream had tricked me.

So now I am waiting for the unveiling of the one true dream, and the pain and the terror bound up with it, the dream of death. I thought long about the loss of my upper left canine, because Angela left me along with this tooth, and I have never been able to accustom myself to this loss.

Five years ago, when I told Angela—naturally in a letter— about the loss of my canine, she did what she had never done in the past decades: she called me on the telephone. She said that all her letters had been sent with only one aim—that of obtaining replies which one day she would be able to burn, with all their beautiful memories. Watching the flames would have been the greatest pain of her life, as I had been the greatest love. She reminded me, whispering words I had written to her once myself, how for weeks and weeks when I was a boy during the war, I'd had only one bit of dry bread to eat a day, with the addition of a little tomato paste. As sucking the tubes of tomato paste had been one of the few true pleasures for me, so depriving herself of the most precious things had been for her. I remember her crying, as she watched my letters burn to ashes. The telephone made the sound of her voice even more agonizing.

That evening I, in turn, burned the letters she had sent me and wept as only a toothless, feeble, aged man can weep. It was not a feeling of deprivation that produced these tears, but the revelation of the permanent condition of man, that of being sans eyes, sans teeth, sans everything. And all the rest an illusion.

Translated from the Italian by Simon Rees

HANIF KUREISHI
WILD WOMEN, WILD MEN

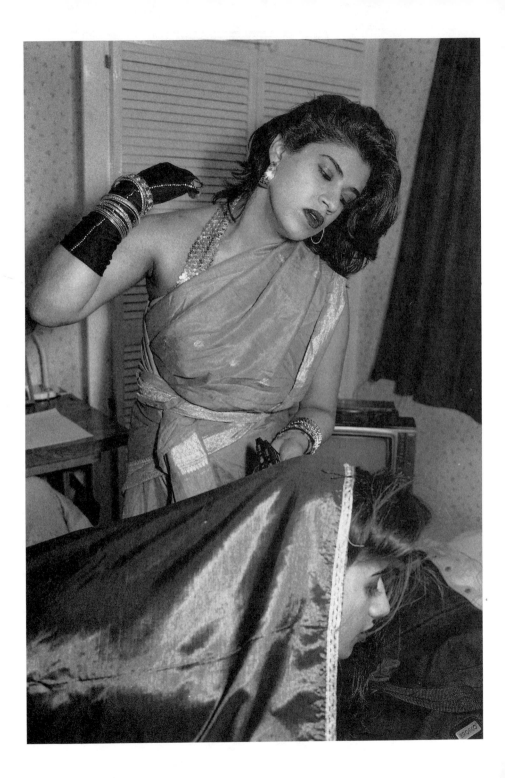

Whenen I saw them waiting beside their car, I said, 'You must be freezing.' It was cold and foggy, the first night of winter, and the two women had matching short skirts and skimpy tops; their legs were bare.

'We wear what we like,' Zarina said.

Zarina was the elder of the pair, at twenty-four. For her this wasn't a job; it was an uprising, mutiny. She was the one with the talent for anarchy and unpredictability that made their show so wild. Qumar was nineteen and seemed more tired and wary. The work could disgust her. And unlike Zarina she did not enjoy the opportunity for mischief and disruption. Qumar had run away from home—her father was a barrister—and worked as a stripper on the Soho circuit, pretending to be Spanish. Zarina had worked as a kissogram. Neither had made much money until they identified themselves as Pakistani Muslims who stripped and did a lesbian double-act. They'd discovered a talent and an audience for it.

The atmosphere was febrile and overwrought. The two women's behaviour was a cross between a pop star's and a fugitive's; they were excited by the notoriety, the money and the danger of what they did. They'd been written up in the *Sport* and the *News of the World*. They wanted me and others to write about them. But everything could get out of hand. The danger was real. It gave their lives an edge, but of the two of them only Qumar knew they were doomed. They had excluded themselves from their community and been condemned. And they hadn't found a safe place among other men and women. Zarina's temperament wouldn't allow her to accept this, though she appeared to be the more nervous. Qumar just knew it would end badly but didn't know how to stop it, perhaps because Zarina didn't want it to stop. And Qumar was, I think, in love with Zarina.

We arrived—in Ealing. A frantic Asian man had been waiting in the drive of a house for two and a half hours. 'Follow my car,' he said. We did: Zarina started to panic.

'We're driving into Southall!' she said. Southall is the heart of Southern England's Asian community, and the women had more enemies here than anywhere else. The Muslim butchers of

173

Southall had threatened their lives and, according to Zarina, had recently murdered a Muslim prostitute by hacking her up and letting her bleed to death, halal style. There could be a butcher concealed in the crowd, Zarina said; and we didn't have any security. It was true: in one car there was the driver and me, and in another there was a female Indian journalist, with two slight Pakistani lads who could have been students.

We came to a row of suburban semi-detached houses with gardens: the street was silent, frozen. If only the neighbours knew. We were greeted by a buoyant middle-aged Muslim man with a round, smiling face. He was clearly anxious but relieved to see us, as he had helped to arrange the evening. It was he, presumably, who had extracted the thirty pounds a head, from which he would pay the girls and take his own cut.

He shook our hands and then, when the front door closed behind us, he snatched at Qumar's arse, pulled her towards him and rubbed his crotch against her. She didn't resist or flinch but she did look away, as if wishing she were somewhere else, as if this wasn't her.

The house was not vulgar, only dingy and virtually bare, with white walls, grimy white plastic armchairs, a brown fraying carpet and a wall-mounted gas fire. The ground floor had been knocked into one long, narrow over-lit room. This unelaborated space was where the women would perform. The upstairs rooms were rented to students.

The men, a third of them Sikh and the rest Muslim, had been waiting for hours and had been drinking. But the atmosphere was benign. No one seemed excited as they stood, many of them in suits and ties, eating chicken curry, black peas and rice from plastic plates. There was none of the aggression of the English lad.

Zarina was the first to dance. Her costume was green and gold, with bells strapped to her ankles; she had placed the big tape-player on the floor beside her. If it weren't for the speed of the music and her jerky, almost inelegant movements, we might have been witnessing a cultural event at the Commonwealth Institute. But Zarina was tense, haughty, unsmiling. She feared Southall. The men stood inches from her, leaning against the

175

wall. They could touch her when they wanted to. And from the moment she began they reached out to pinch or stroke her. But they didn't know what Zarina might do in return.

At the end of the room stood a fifty-year-old six-foot Sikh, an ecstatic look on his face, swaying to the music, wiggling his hips at Zarina. Zarina, who was tiny but strong and fast, suddenly ran at the Sikh, threateningly, as if she were going to tackle him. She knocked into him, but he didn't fall, and she then appeared to be climbing up him. She wrestled off his tweed jacket and threw it down. He complied. He was enjoying this. He pulled off his shirt and she dropped to her knees, jerking down his trousers and pants. His stomach fell out of his clothes—suddenly, like a suitcase falling off the top of a wardrobe. The tiny button of his penis shrank. Zarina wrapped her legs around his waist and beat her hands on his shoulders. The Sikh danced, and the others clapped and cheered. Then he plucked off his turban and threw it into the air, a balding man with his few strands of hair drawn into a frizzy bun.

Zarina was then grabbed from behind. It was the mild, buoyant man who had greeted us at the door. He pulled his trousers off and stood in his blue and white spotted boxer shorts. He began to gyrate against Zarina.

And then she was gone, slipping away as if greased from the bottom of the scrum, out of the door and upstairs to Qumar. The music ended, and the big Sikh, still naked, was putting his turban back on. Another Sikh looked at him disapprovingly; a younger one laughed. The men fetched more drinks. They were pleased and exhilarated, as if they'd survived a fight. The door-greeter walked around in his shorts and shoes.

After a break, Zarina and Qumar returned for another set, this time in black bra and pants. The music was even faster. I noticed that the door-greeter was in a strange state. He had been relaxed, even a little glazed, but now, as the women danced, he was rigid with excitement, chattering to the man next to him, and then to himself, until finally his words became a kind of chant. 'We are hypocrite Muslims,' he was saying. 'We are hypocrite Muslims,'—again and again, causing the man near him to move away.

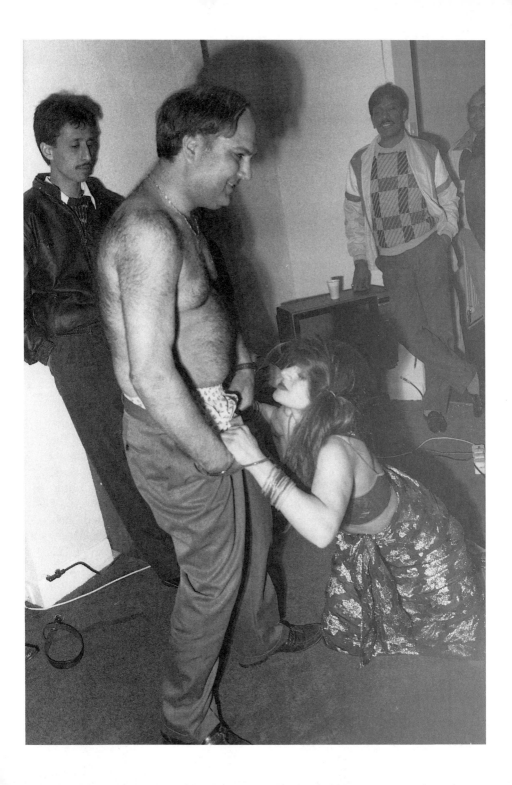

Zarina's assault on the Sikh and on some of the other, more reluctant men had broken that line that separated spectator from performer. The men had come to see the women. They hadn't anticipated having their pants pulled around their ankles and their cocks revealed to other men. But it was Zarina's intention to round on the men, not turn them on—to humiliate and frighten them. This was part of the act.

The confirmed spectators were now grouped in the kitchen behind a table; the others joined in on the floor. Qumar and Zarina removed their tops. The young and friendly man who owned the house was sitting next to me, exultant. He thought I was the women's manager and he said in my ear: 'They are fantastic, this is out of this world! I have never seen anything like this before—what a beef! Get me two more girls for Wednesday and four for Saturday.' But things were getting out of hand. The centre of the room was starting to resemble a playground fight, a bundle, a children's party. The landlord, panicking, was attempting to separate the men and the two women. He told me to help.

An older man, another Sikh, the oldest man in the room, had been sitting in an armchair from which he reached out occasionally to nip Zarina's breasts. But now he was on the floor—I don't know how—and Zarina was on his head. Qumar was squatting on his stomach with her hand inside his trousers. It didn't seem like a game any more, and people were arguing. The landlord was saying to me, 'This man, he's a respectable man, he's the richest man, one of the best known in Southall, he's an old man . . . ' Zarina and Qumar were stripping him. Other men, having lost their tempers, were attempting to drag the women away.

The old man was helped to his feet. He was breathing heavily, as if about to have a seizure. He was trying to stop himself from crying. His turban had been dislodged and chicken curry and rice had been smeared over him, which he was trying to brush off.

There was still the final part of the show. For this, the men sat cross-legged on the floor to watch the women pretend to have sex with each other. One man got down on his knees as if he were checking his car exhaust-pipe—and peered up Zarina's cunt. Beside me, the landlord was passing comment once more. Our Muslim girls don't usually shave themselves, he said. He disapproved of the neatly trimmed black strip of hair over Zarina's cunt.

The show lasted over two hours. 'It wasn't difficult,' Qumar said. They were exhausted. They would ache and be covered in bruises. They did two shows a week.

THE ONLY BRITISH MAGAZINE FOR MEN   SPRING 92 MARCH/APRIL £2

ARENA

Triple Whammy!
Extract from the
new Carl Hiaasen

Food & Sex
What's on the menu

**Dallas
in the desert**
Douglas Kennedy
in Dubai

Love in the time of HIV
By Tony Parsons

**Goodfellas
with bad reputations**
Robert Mitchum
Oliver Reed
Nik Cohn
Lou Reed
Robert Elms

Ray Liotta

The Tyson factor: introducing the ARENA sports column
Spring fashion: trends, classics, previews

A/32   RAY LIOTTA PHOTOGRAPHED BY NAOMI KALTMAN

ARENA

THE ONLY BRITISH MAGAZINE FOR MEN

NEW ISSUE ON SALE NOW £2

ANTONIN KRATOCHVIL
SIDESHOW

Antonin Kratochvil took these photographs in the late seventies. The performers in 'Sideshow' toured America in the summer and spent the winter in Florida. Some of them were accident victims with no medical insurance, who supported themselves by appearing in the show (Ray, page 186, lost his legs in a railway crash). Others were circus performers (the sword-swallower also swallowed fluorescent light-bulbs, until one exploded in his stomach). Chris Walker (page 188) had fought in the Korean War. He suffered from post-traumatic stress disorder and tried to kill himself by overeating, until he began making his living as 'the fattest man in the world' (he was not entered in the *Guinness Book of Records*—the approved scales were too small for him to use).

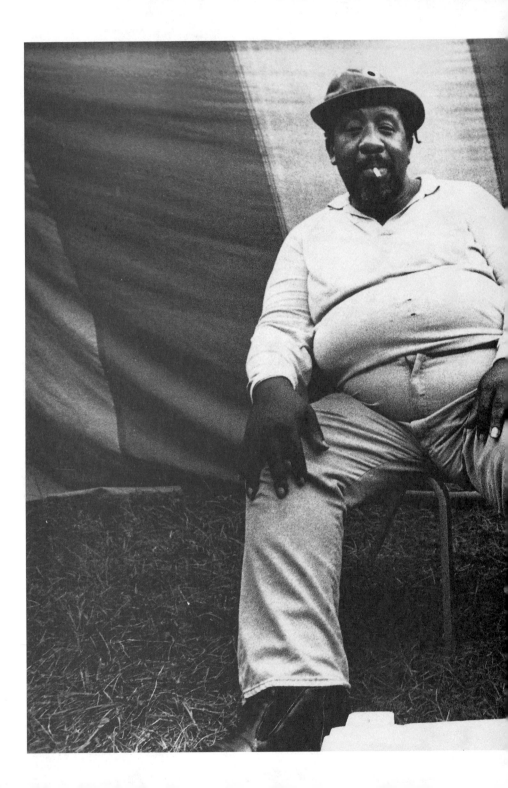

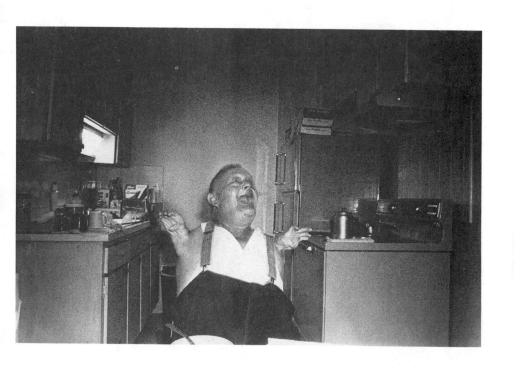

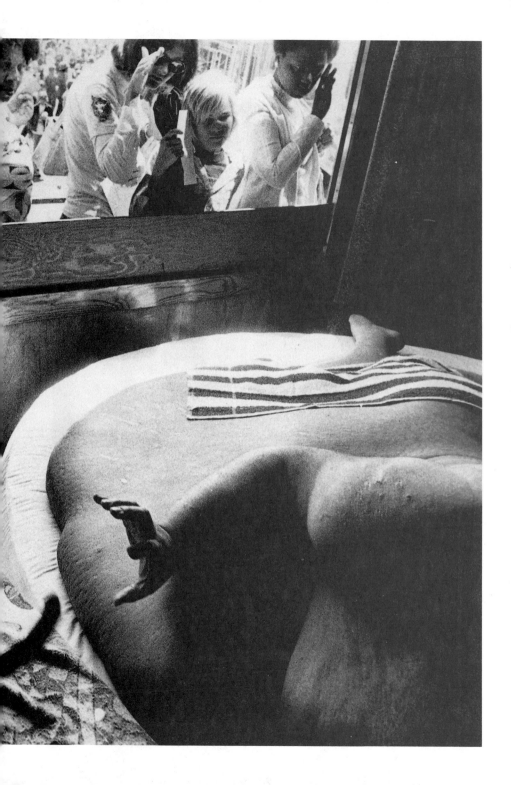

SOUL FOOD

BETWEEN THOUGHT AND EXPRESSION

Selected Lyrics of Lou Reed
A collection of sharp-edged social criticism and shrewd observation by the legendary guitarist, vocalist and songwriter.

DEAD ELVIS

A Chronicle of a Cultural Obsession
Greil Marcus '*No one tracks Elvis Presley's bizarre journey through the American psyche more imaginatively and perceptively than Greil Marcus.*' Charles Shaar Murray

THE VERY MODEL OF A MAN

Howard Jacobson
To the wit and energy of his previous novels Howard Jacobson brings a poignancy, an anguished laughter of the soul, that makes this re-telling of the Cain and Abel story a divine comedy of the darkest shade. *Published 30 April*

THE PENGUIN BOOK OF LATIN AMERICAN SHORT STORIES

Edited by Thomas Colchie
This anthology celebrates some of the most exciting authors in contemporary literature, including contributions by Jorge Luís Borges, Isabel Allende, Manuel Puig, Carlos Fuentes and Gabriel García Márquez.

VIKING

ANCHEE MIN
RED FIRE FARM

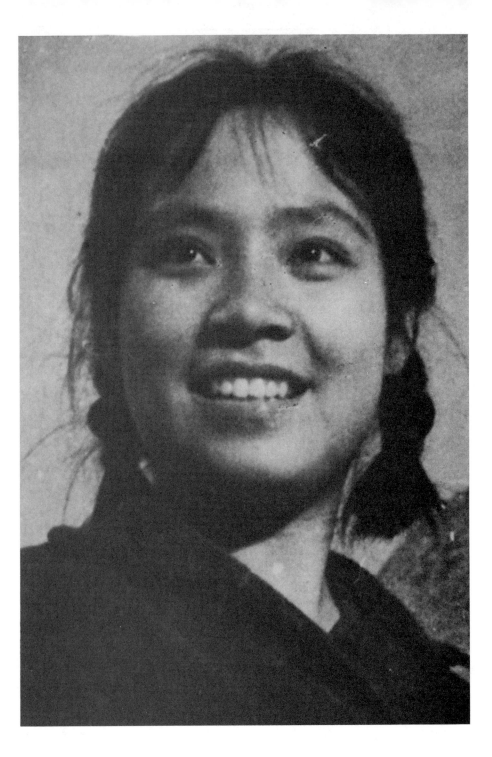

I arrived at Red Fire Farm—along with many other girls in ten large trucks—late one spring afternoon in 1974. Our names had appeared on our schools' Glorious Red Lists, a great honour, but one which meant that we would have to leave home to work in another province. The farm was near the East China Sea. It consisted of endless fields of sea reeds, and rectangular grey barracks each with a long outdoor sink.

I was assigned to house number three, and to a small room with bunk beds for my seven room-mates. The floor was packed earth. My only private space was provided by a mosquito net that hung from thin bamboo sticks. The bed next to mine was given to a girl named Shao Ching, who, like me, was seventeen years old. Shao Ching was pale-skinned and slim as a willow. When she spoke, she looked down at the ground. Unlike the rest of us who tied our braids with standard brown rubber-bands, Shao Ching tied hers with colourful strings. She was extremely neat. No matter how tired we got after a day's heavy labour, she would walk forty-five minutes to the hot-water station and then carry back water to wash herself.

I was proud to be Shao Ching's friend. She showed me how she used remnants of fabric to make pretty underwear, finely embroidered with flowers, leaves and love-birds. She hung a string next to the little window between our beds on which she could hang her underwear to dry. In our bare room the string was like an art gallery.

All the girls secretly envied Shao Ching. She redesigned the clothes she was issued: her shirts to taper at the waist; her trousers to make her legs look longer. She was not embarrassed by her full breasts. The male soldiers stared at her whenever she passed by and when the weather got hotter, she dared to go without a bra. There was one man who was said to have burst into tears on hearing that Shao Ching was running a high fever.

I had become friends with Shao Ching on our first day in the rice fields. A leech had bitten her, and when she went to pull it out it had burrowed into her skin, leaving only a black dot on the surface. I was working alongside her; when she screamed, I called

Anchee Min, Red Fire Farm, 1975.

A-Lan, an experienced soldier, who showed us how we should pat the skin above the leech's head so that it would back itself out.

W̶e had been greeted at the farm—as we got down from the trucks on that first afternoon—by the Company Commander, Yan. She was about twenty-three, tall, well-built, and walked with authority. She wore an old People's Liberation Army uniform, washed white and gathered at the waist with a three-inch-wide belt. Her hair was plaited into two short, thick braids. She had examined us one by one, then begun to speak in a whisper, introducing herself—'My name is Yan Sheng. Yan meaning discipline; Sheng, victory'—welcoming us, and then shouting suddenly, 'I have only one thing to say: Don't any of you shit on my face! Don't any of you betray the glorious name of the Advanced Seventh Company, model of the entire Red Fire Farm Army!' She'd asked if she had made her point clear.

Startled, we had answered, 'Yes!'

My platoon leader, a bearded man called Lin, was a great admirer of Yan. During a break from work in the fields, he told us how Yan had been accepted as a member of the Party at the age of nineteen. When she had arrived five years ago, he said, the land of Red Fire Farm had been barren. She had led her platoon of twenty Red Guards in reclaiming it. Lin had been among them.

'Yan is famous for her iron shoulders,' he said. 'We all had blisters when we were working on irrigation channels. To remove the mud, we had to make at least twenty half-mile-trips in a day, carrying over a hundred and sixty pounds in two hods hanging from a shoulder-pole. Our shoulders swelled like steamed bread. Strong men like me gave up. Yan was a thin girl at that time, but she did not quit. She continued carrying the hods of mud and her blisters bled.'

In my first days at the farm, I had seen Yan carry large loads. She had piled reed upon reed upon her head until she looked like she had a hill on her shoulders, with only her legs moving underneath.

Lin mentioned a fire from the last summer. 'Our grain stores, straw-huts and fields of ripe crops,' he said, 'were destroyed. Soldiers cried. But Yan stood in front of us. One of her braids had burnt off and her clothes were smoking; she told us that our faith in Communism was all we needed to rebuild our dream. We built these houses in five months . . . '

I imagined Yan with a burnt off braid, her skin scorched by fire raging behind her. I had always admired the heroines in the revolutionary operas created by Madam Mao, Comrade Jiang Ching.

Without being aware of it, in a few weeks, I started to imitate Yan. My belt was only two inches wide; I wished it was an inch wider. I cut my long braids short. I tried to carry as much as I could when our platoon was sent to dig a new irrigation channel, even tried to allow my shoulder-pole to rub my bleeding blisters, though the pain was unbearable. And every night I gave speeches at meetings for confession and self-criticism.

At one of these meetings Yan raised an important matter. It concerned Shao Ching. Two of her prettiest hand-embroidered pairs of underwear had been stolen from the line between our beds. The platoon leader suspected the male soldiers and had reported the case to the Party Committee. No one had admitted to the theft. Yan's deputy, a fierce woman named Lu, said that such behaviour shamed us all. She criticized Shao Ching for vanity and ordered her to make a confession. Yan told Shao Ching that in future she should not hang her underwear near to the window.

After some months on the farm, a group of us were selected for military training programmes. I was among them. We were given tuition in shooting, handling grenades, and combat. We were also called on 'midnight emergency searches' when we had to pull ourselves out of the bed and be ready to leave with our rifles and flashlights in three minutes.

One night in early summer, the platoon leader called for me at my window and within minutes I was off with the group. There was a warm, gentle breeze. We moved briskly, almost jogging, through the reeds. When we reached the wheat fields, an order was given in a whisper: 'Load!'

I snapped awake—this was the first order to use live ammunition—something serious had happened. I loaded my gun.

'Lie down!' I heard Yan's voice. 'Advance!'

We began crawling through the wheat. It was hard to see. The male soldier in front of me stopped crawling and passed back an order, 'Stand by!'

I lay there holding my breath, listening. The insects were singing and the wheat smelled sweet. Mosquitoes began to bite me through my clothes. There was a noise in the distance. Then silence. I thought the noise had been my imagination. After about a minute, I heard the noise again. It was two sounds. One was a man's, the other was a woman murmuring. I heard a soft, muted cry. And then my shock: I recognized the voice as Shao Ching's.

My only thought was: I can't let Shao Ching be caught like this. She was my best friend, the only person in my room who was open with me. She had never told me anything about being involved with a man, though I could understand why: it would be shameful to admit. A good female comrade was supposed to devote all her energy, her youth, to the Revolution; she was not permitted even to think about a man until she reached her late twenties, when marriage would be considered. I thought of the consequences Shao Ching would have to bear if she were caught. I crawled forward towards the noise. A firm hand immediately pressed me down to the ground. Yan. She seemed to know exactly what was going on.

As the murmuring and hard breathing became louder, I heard Yan clench her teeth together and draw in a breath, then she loosened her grip on my back and shouted suddenly, 'Now!'

It was as if a bomb had exploded next to me. Yan turned her flashlight on Shao Ching and the man. About thirty other flashlights, including mine, were switched on at the same time.

Shao Ching screamed. She was in her favourite shirt—the one embroidered with pink mei flowers. The lights shone on her naked buttocks.

The man with Shao Ching was skinny, wore glasses and looked very bookish. He pulled up his pants and tried to run. He was caught immediately by the group led by the deputy commander, Lu, who pulled out her rifle, and held it to the bookish man's head. He wasn't from our company, but I remembered having seen him at the market. He had smiled at Shao Ching, but when I had asked whether she knew him, she had said no.

Shao Ching was trembling and weeping. She scrambled back and forth for her clothes, trying to cover her buttocks with her hands.

I lowered my flashlight.

Yan slowly approached the man, 'Why do you have to do this?' To my surprise, I saw that her eyes glistened with tears.

The man bit his lip.

Yan threw her belt down and ordered the male soldiers to beat the man. She walked away but stopped and said, 'I'll be pleased if you can make him understand that today's woman is no longer the victim of man's desire.' She took off her jacket to cover Shao Ching. 'Let's go home,' she said softly.

The bookish man didn't look guilty. As the kicking and whipping began, he struggled not to cry out.

I returned to the barracks with the other female soldiers. From a distance we could hear muted cries from the man and Lu shouting, 'Death to the rapist!' Shao Ching could not stop whimpering.

A public trial was held in the dining-hall. Shao Ching had undergone four days of 'intensive mind re-brushing'. On a makeshift stage, she declared in a high, strained voice that she had been raped. The paper from which she read slipped out of her hands twice. Her bookish lover was convicted. I will never forget his expression when the death sentence was announced. As if waking from a nightmare, he looked suddenly relaxed. His bruised purple face had brightened when Shao Ching walked into the hall.

No one talked about the man after the execution, although he was on everyone's mind. But Shao Ching had changed. She stopped washing. Months passed. Still she hadn't washed. There were complaints about her smell. When I tried to persuade her to wash her underwear at least, she took a pair of scissors and cut it into strips. She chopped off her long braids and stopped combing her hair. Mucus dripped from her lips. At night, she sang songs off-key. My room-mates reported her behaviour and she was sent to the farm's hospital. The doctors referred her to a hospital in Shanghai where she was diagnosed as having had a nervous breakdown.

When Shao Ching returned from hospital six months later, I didn't recognize her. The drugs she had been prescribed had made her gain weight. She was as fat as a bear.

She was again given a bed in my room, where she sat quietly most of the day, staring in one direction. Her pupils sometimes moved upwards, then disappeared into her skull as if she was trying to read her own brain. Her hair was matted. I thought of the evenings when she would wash her hair after dinner, and comb and dry it as the sun set. She used to sing 'My Mother Land', a song that we all knew.

There are girls like beautiful flowers,
Boys with strong bodies and open minds.
To build our new China,
We are happily working and sweating together . . .

I spent the night of my eighteenth birthday under my mosquito net. I had a small mirror and used it to examine my body. I was restless. I had begun having thoughts about men and I felt disgusted with myself.

'Learn to have a stainless mind!' was a popular slogan at the time. The model women used in propaganda never had men. The heroines in the revolutionary operas had neither husbands nor lovers. The heroine in my life, Yan, didn't seem to have anything to do with men either. Did she feel restless? How did she feel about her body? Recently, she seemed more serious than before, and more irritable. She had tried several times to talk to Shao Ching. Each time she had been left staring at Shao Ching with a confused expression.

In the late evenings I saw Yan setting out alone for the fields. When I followed her I found that she was trying to catch poisonous water-snakes in the reeds. When she caught one she put it in a jar she carried. I did not have the courage to ask what she was doing.

2

In the early hours of the morning the rain had started. The clothes I put out to dry before going to bed were wet and muddy. I took them down from the string and put them on, then dragged myself to the field. We were transplanting rice shoots. We worked for three hours without a break. I was working the edge of the field and noticed a trace of blood in the muddy water. I tracked the blood and found A-Lan, the woman who had shown us how to remove leeches, down on her knees in the water, her pants bloody red. A-Lan always had problems with her period. It could last for half a month, bleeding her to exhaustion. She told me that she hadn't understood what her period was when it first came. She felt too ashamed to ask anyone for advice and stuffed unsterilized clothes into her pants to try to block the blood. She became infected. I asked her why she hadn't told her mother or a friend about it.

'My mother was in a labour camp,' she said. 'My friend knew even less than me. She once asked me if Chairman Mao was a man or a woman.'

Why hadn't she asked the platoon leader for a day off?

'I did,' said A-Lan, 'but I was rejected. The head sent me to Lu and Lu said that the transplanting had to be completed by midnight or we would lose the season.'

I told A-Lan that I would help her as soon as I finished my own planting.

The rain became heavier. I worked fast so I could go to help A-Lan, my arms and fingers moving as if they were not mine. Standing to stretch my back, I noticed Yan a few plots away. She moved like a dancer: passing the rice shoots from left hand to right and inserting the shoots into the mud in perfect time with her steps backward. Her wet clothes were pasted to her body.

I did my best to compete, Yan responded to the challenge. She sped up and I fell far behind; then suddenly slowed down to allow me to catch up, before surging ahead again. She finished with one plot, then went on to the next without turning her head.

The sky turned dark. A loudspeaker broadcast live interviews with labour heroes and encouraged everybody to make a final effort. Two huge bright lights were carried to the fields, and steamed bread was brought out. A-Lan was in tears when I finally went to help her, and a long way behind. We chewed our bread while we planted the shoots. We finished at ten o'clock.

A-Lan thanked me, crying with relief, 'My mother would have killed herself if she had seen me working like this . . . '

As we left the field, a meeting was called. One of the lights was being moved to the plot where we had worked, millions of mosquitoes swarming into its ray. Lin, our platoon leader, shouted for our attention. 'We need to talk about the quality of our day's work. Here is the Commander.'

He passed the loudspeaker to Yan, who was coated with mud. Only her eyes were sparkling. She ordered for the light to be moved to illuminate a particular spot where dozens of rice shoots were floating on the water. 'Someone did a nice job here!' Yan said, 'The shoots will all be dead before daybreak.'

The soldiers began to survey the fields nervously. The word broke out that the section responsible for the careless planting was platoon number four—our territory. I recognized that it was the area I had worked as I tried to keep up with Yan.

Lu ordered that the person responsible should step out of the ranks. A-Lan sensed my fear, and grabbed my hand tightly.

'No one leaves until the mistake is admitted,' said Lu.

As I gathered all my courage and was about to step out, Yan suddenly said, 'Well, I prefer to let the comrade correct his own mistake. Understood?'

'Yes!' the soldiers called.

The fields had become quiet in the moonlight. The drizzle had stopped and the air was still. I planted my feet in the mud and began to redo the work, singing a Chairman Mao quotation song to fight off sleep, 'Made up my mind, not to fear death; overcome all the difficulties, and strive for victory. Made up my mind . . . '

The sky was piled with orange clouds when I woke. The sun was yet to rise. I sat up looking around, knowing I hadn't finished the work. But I saw that it had been done. Was I dreaming? As I looked towards the sun, there was someone, about thirty yards away pacing the field.

It was Yan. After she was done, she washed her hands in the irrigation channel. 'A-Lan came to me last night and told me everything,' she said, unknotting her hair, then bending to wash it in the channel. She combed her hair with her fingers and braided it. 'When I found you,' she said, 'you looked like a big turtle lying in the field. I thought you were dead.' She paused. 'I felt guilty.'

I rubbed my eyes.

'You are strong willed.' She looked me in the eyes, a thread of a smile on her face. After a while she got up and said, 'I want you to be the leader of platoon number four. Move in with me so we can discuss the company problem together.' She walked quickly back to the barracks.

I moved in with Yan and six other platoon heads. Yan and I shared a bunk bed, I occupied the top. The room was the same size as the room I had lived in before. It served as bedroom, dining-room and conference-room. It was also a battle front: for although Yan was officially in charge, Lu was obsessed with power.

I always took Yan's side when they fought. After Lu had tried to 'cultivate' me as an advanced-activist of her own 'special study team,' and I had showed my disinterest, she saw me as a stone in her shoe. 'If one doesn't come to her political senses, one might lose her future,' she reminded me.

I cared about my political image and I wanted to look noble to the others. To make Yan proud, I often picked the hardest labour task for my platoon. At the end of the year we were given a citation and I was accepted by the Communist Youth League. At the ceremony, Yan walked on the stage to congratulate me. She took my hands and squeezed them in her thick, carrot-like finger joints. Laughing, she whispered that she couldn't wait to have me join the Party. For many nights afterward, before going to sleep, I replayed the ceremony in my head. I dreamt of Yan's laughter.

After the busy summer season ended, the soldiers were allowed a little time to themselves after dinner. The spare time made my heart feel empty. I missed Shao Ching terribly. I combed her hair and washed her clothes. Although her body was getting back to its shape—she was once again slim like a willow—her mind seemed to have gone for ever. Nothing I tried made her respond to me. She still wore the shirt with mei flower on it—the one she had on the night she was caught—but it had holes under the armpits and at the elbows. The shirt reminded me of the night—I'll never forget it—when I had my gun pointed at her. Shao Ching had become dangerous to herself. Once I caught her swallowing stones. I reported the incident to Yan. From then on, I often saw Yan following her around the fields in late evenings; they were like two boats drifting over the sea in a dense fog.

3

I began to dislike going into my mosquito net. It was too quiet. I avoided my bed and walked the narrow paths through the reeds. One night, I found myself at the farm's brick factory. Thousands of ready-to-bake bricks were laid out in patterns. Some stacks were eight feet high, some leaning as if about to fall, and some had already fallen. I could hear the echo of my own steps. The place had the feel of an ancient ruin.

There was another sound among the bricks, like the noise of an erhu, a two-stringed lute. I picked out the melody—'Liang and Zhu', from a banned Chinese opera, my grandmother used to hum it. I loved the ending of that opera: Liang and Zhu, the two lovers who commit suicide are transformed into butterflies. It surprised me to hear someone on the farm able to play it with such skill.

I followed the sound. It stopped. I heard steps and found the erhu on a brick stool. As I bent over to pick up the instrument a pair of hands came from behind me and covered my eyes.

'Who is this?' I asked.

No reply.

I reached back to tickle the body behind me. There was a giggle, a hot breath on my neck. 'Yan?'

She stood in front of me, smiling, and I felt a sudden joy.

She sat on the brick stool and motioned me to sit next to her. I wanted to tell her how beautifully she played. Still smiling, saying nothing, she picked up the erhu and the bow, retuned the strings, bent her head toward the instrument and closed her eyes. She started to play a tune called 'The River'. Her fingers ran up and down on the strings. When she stopped the notes, she held her breath. Then she slowly inhaled as her finger-tip plucked the string. The stronger notes were wrenched out violently. She raised her head with her eyes closed and chin tilted up: the Party Secretary, the heroine, and the erhu player . . . She played 'Horse Racing', 'The Red Army Brother Is Coming Back', and finally, at my request, she played 'Liang and Zhu' again.

We talked. We told each other our life stories. In our eagerness to express ourselves we overlapped each other's sentences.

Yan's parents were textile workers. Her mother had been honoured as a 'Glory Mother' in the fifties for producing nine children. Yan was the eighth. They lived in one wood-framed room and shared a well with twenty other families. They had no toilet, only a wooden shit container. Yan took the container to a public sewage depot every morning to clean it.

Her parents loved folk music; they saved their money and bought Yan an erhu for her tenth birthday. They hoped that Yan would one day become a famous erhu player.

Yan was fifteen years old when the Cultural Revolution began in 1966. She joined the Red Guard and marched to Beijing to be inspected by Chairman Mao at Tiananmen Square. As the youngest Red Guard representative, she was invited to watch an opera. She fell in love with the three-inch-wide belts the performers were wearing. 'I traded a belt with one of the performers for my best collection of Mao buttons,' she said. She showed me her belt, made of real leather and copper. 'The performer told me it was designed by Comrade Jiang Ching.' She said she had read every book of Mao's, had memorized the Little Red Book and knew every quotation song.

I began to sing, 'The Party runs by good policies . . . '

'Page seven, second paragraph!' she said loudly.

'If the broom doesn't come, the garbage won't automatically go away . . . '

'Page ten, first paragraph!'
'The world is yours . . . '
'Page two hundred and sixty-three, first paragraph!'
'Studying Chairman Mao's works, we must learn to be efficient. We should apply his teachings to our problems to ensure a fast result . . . '
Yan joined my singing, 'as when we erect a bamboo stick in the sunshine, we see the shadow right away . . . '
'Where are we?' I shouted.
'Vice Chairman Lin Bioa's *Preface For Mao Quotation*, second edition!' Yan shouted back, and we laughed with great joy.
We were still talking when we reached our barracks. We stood in the dark, filled with delight.

After that night, as if by secret arrangement, Yan and I betrayed no intimacy in public. We silently washed each other's clothes and took trips to fill hot-water containers for each other. We became accustomed to each other's eye signals. Every couple of weeks, we would go separately to visit our 'ruins'. Yan would make excuses such as 'checking the quality of the day's work.' I would take the thickest of Mao's books and my notebook and pretend to find a place to study by myself.

Even when winter came, we didn't stop meeting. Yan would practice her erhu; I would just lie back and listen. We began to talk about everything, including that most forbidden subject— men.

Yan said that according to her mother, who hated her father, most men were evil. 'Mother said that she wouldn't have ever produced nine children with my father if she had not wanted to respond to the Party's call. Men take pleasure in seducing and raping women,' she concluded.

I remembered how Yan had taken off her belt that night and ordered the male soldiers to beat the bookish man—and I told Yan that I had hated her for exposing Shao Ching.

Yan lowered her head and listened to my accusation quietly. I cried. Yan said that she hated herself too. She had known for a long time that Lu had been spying on Shao Ching. As the Party

206

Secretary and Commander, she had no choice when the case was reported. She took my hands in hers and rubbed them. Her hands were rough, like those of an old farmer. 'Don't worry,' Yan said, gazing at the sunset, 'Shao Ching will recover one day.' She then told me that she had collected sixty-nine water-snakes in a jar which she stored under our bed: the snakes I had seen her catching in the reeds.

'This is the first time in my life I've put faith in superstitions,' she said. 'My grandmother once collected snakes to cure her disabled sister. When she had one hundred, her sister stood up and walked. She had been paralysed for six years.'

When Yan asked me how I felt about men, I told her a story I had never told anyone. It had happened during a Red Guards' meeting when I was seventeen. There had been a power cut and as we were waiting in the dark, a hand touched my back. Trembling, it slowly moved around my side to touch my breast. I allowed the hand to stay there for about a minute then stood up and moved to another seat. When the lights came back on I turned to see three boys, all about my age. I knew one of them—a straight-A student with a girlish face. He looked nervous and pale.

'Why didn't you yell,' Yan asked.

I told her that actually my body had felt good.

Yan looked stunned. She sat in silence for a while. Then, blushing, she told me she had something to confess.

I waited.

She took a breath and said she couldn't, then rested her head on her knees.

I pulled her knees apart and lifted her chin.

His name was Fong Chen, she said, he was head of Company thirty-two and she had met him at the headquarters meeting two months ago.

I asked if they had talked, and Yan said they hadn't.

'Well, how do you know he likes you?'

She just felt that he did, she said.

'Oh! What a personal life corruption!' I said. 'Please raise this problem at the Company meeting.'

She told me to stop joking, she was worried, I had to help her.

I said I would lend her *The Second-time Handshake*—a banned book that Shao Ching had copied and lent to me when she had first arrived at the farm.

Yan read the book in three nights at the brick factory. When she returned the copy to me, she seemed inspired. She wanted to write to Fong Chen. Then her face fell. Yan explained how Lu had intercepted and read Shao Ching's love letters; that was how they had known she would be in the field that night. 'I can't do things I have forbidden others to do.'

I argued that if she now understood that what she had done to Shao Ching was wrong, why should she repeat the mistake?

That night, on our way home, we discussed how the letter should be written, and how I could find an official excuse to deliver it to Fong Chen.

Two weeks passed, and Yan had not given me anything to deliver. Then one night, when I was lying in bed, she opened my curtain and threw in a folded letter:

Comrade Fong Chen

How are you? I was wondering how the agricultural initiative is progressing in your company. Here we are making good progress.

I have thought of our meeting often. It was meaningful, as well as politically fruitful.

In the margin Yan had written, 'Will you please help.' I took a piece of paper and replied that I would do whatever the Party required of me. The next day I rewrote her letter. I didn't know what Fong looked like so I described Yan's face instead. I tried to imagine how they would touch each other; just thinking of it made my heart beat fast. I wanted to describe Yan's body, but I had never seen it. I described my own instead, touching myself and imagining my body were hers and my fingers his.

When Yan returned, I whispered that I had finished. We told Lu—who was up as usual studying Mao—that because it was so cold we would sleep in the same bed and share blankets. Yan pulled them up over us and turned on her flashlight. I watched as her face flushed. She re-read the letter three times. Through the mosquito net I saw Lu stand up and turn out the light. Yan wanted me to imagine how Fong would react to the letter. I whispered that he would be unable to stop thinking of her. We lay awake in the dark, too excited to sleep.

Yan turned away from me and sighed; she seemed to be murmuring something.

Our room-mates were breathing evenly, Lu was snoring.

Yan sighed again, 'Too bad,' she said, 'that you are not a man.'

I asked what she would do if I were.

Her breath was hot. She said she would do exactly as I had described in the letter.

We lay in silence. She put one of her legs between mine. Our arms were around each other. Then almost at the same time we pulled away. The snakes were beating against the sides of the jar under the bed.

I delivered four letters to Fong in two months. He never wrote back. In order to share a bed with Yan, I continued to complain of the cold. She did not wash her mosquito net because the dirt made it less transparent. When the light was on, no one was able to see us.

I enjoyed seeing Yan flush when she read my letters. I asked her to imagine herself being loved by Fong, insisting on detail that I could use the next time I wrote. Yan would grin and say I was embarrassing her. One day she grabbed my hand and pressed it to her chest telling me to feel how I was driving her to a heart attack. Her heart was hammering. She was wearing a thin shirt with a bra under it. Her lips were parted slightly. I heard Lu's cough. She was sitting three feet away at the table concentrating on Mao. She turned a page. Yan closed her eyes and moved my fingers up to caress her face. I made an effort to look away, staring at the ceiling. Yan put her arms around my neck so that her breasts were pressed against my shoulder. She untied one of her braids then helped me to untie the other so that I could smooth the loose hair with my fingers. Lu was now brushing her teeth. She spat outside, then came in and turned out the light.

The bed frame shook as she climbed in. I waited for her snoring. Yan began to whisper in my ear, reciting some of the phrases I had used in my letters.

4

One day in spring I took my platoon to repair a bridge. By four o'clock I was able to dismiss them. The members of my platoon liked me. My policy was unique—when the assignment was completed they were allowed to take the rest of the day off. In many cases, those who finished the work would stay to help other platoons, in response to my call 'to carry forward the communist collaborative spirit.' Lu didn't like my policy; she called it 'capitalist contract bullshit'. She had asked me to change it and I had no choice but to acquiesce. But when she wasn't inspecting, I did things my way.

When the work was done I walked across the bridge. Along the canal side there was a huge slogan painted on canvas and mounted on thick bamboo sticks which said 'Do not fear death or hard work.' We had created the canal ourselves that winter. I felt proud every time I walked by it.

This particular day, as I passed by the bridge I heard a local boatman calling me from his boat. He told me to come quickly; he had discovered a drowned body. I ran down to the boat. It was a female body. The boatman slowly flipped it over like an egg-roll on a skillet. In front of me was Shao Ching. I lost my breath. Her face was puffed. The whole head had swelled like a pumpkin. There were traces of cuts on her arms and legs.

'It looks like she had a fit,' the boatman said. 'You see these cuts? She struggled, but got tangled in the weeds.'

I stood there motionless.

Someone got the news to Yan. She came running down from the bridge like a mad horse with her hair standing back on its roots. Her face was blue and red as if it had been beaten. She wouldn't listen when the boatman told her that it was useless to attempt mouth-to-mouth life-saving. 'She's been dead for hours,' the boatman said. Yan kept pumping and pumping at Shao

Ching's chest. Heavy sweat ran down her hair in tiny streams. Her shirt was soon soaked. She didn't stop until she completely exhausted herself.

The Red Fire Farm headquarters held a special memorial service for Shao Ching. She was honoured as an 'Outstanding Comrade,' and was admitted posthumously into the Youth League of the Communist Party. Shao Ching's grandmother attended the service. She was very beautiful which reminded us of the way Shao Ching used to be. Lu, representing the farm's Party Committee, issued her a cheque for 500 yuan as a condolence.

Before the service ended, Yan left suddenly. She didn't come back for dinner. I went to look for her, searching everywhere, before I finally found her sitting under the bridge. The jar which she used to collect the snakes was placed next to her. A few days before she had told me in great delight that she had just reached the perfect number—one hundred snakes—and was expecting Shao Ching to come back to her senses magically.

I stepped closer to watch Yan and saw that she was pulling each snake's head off its neck. The dark brown blood of the snakes spattered all over her face and uniform. When all the snakes were torn, she took up the jar and smashed it.

I went up to her. She crouched at my knees. I held her as she began to cry.

THE
MODERN REVIEW

Spring 1992   Volume 1   Issue 3

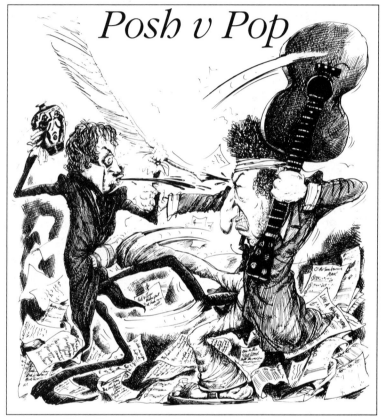

Posh v Pop

why Dylan is better than Keats

SUBSCRIPTION FORM

Name ....

Address ....

....

....

G1
Please enter my subscription
for six issues. I enclose a
cheque for £10.00 (Europe
£14.00, USA $35.00) made
payable to *The Modern Review*.
All correspondence to:

**The Modern Review,
6 Hopgood Street,
London W12 7JU.**

JOHN CONROY
THE INTERNMENT

In a low-rent corner of Belfast's city centre is a district known as Smithfield, and on its main street there is a market, an anarchist bookshop, a public toilet and a bookmaker's called Stanley's. Above Stanley's is the office of Challenge for Youth, an organization that provides support for teenagers in trouble. One afternoon in January last year, I went there to meet Jim Auld, the head of the operation.

He was just turning forty, although I would have guessed he was older—his hair and beard were greying. Twenty years earlier, he was arrested in the middle of the night, taken to a secret location and tortured. He was one of fourteen Northern Irish Catholic men who were tortured on the orders of the British government, which for the past two decades has concealed the identities of the torturers, their commanding officers and the men at the highest levels of government who sanctioned the abuse.

In the summer of 1971, Edward Heath, then Prime Minister, approved plans to introduce internment in Northern Ireland, a policy which empowered the government to arrest and hold anyone without charge for an unlimited period. Army intelligence officers compiled a list of potential internees: over five hundred Catholics whom they believed to be IRA members and sympathizers, plus civil rights activists who would organize protests if internment were introduced. Before dawn on 9 August 1971, the army began making arrests. By nightfall, 342 Catholics were in custody. The army's intelligence proved to be so unreliable that almost a third of those arrested were released within forty-eight hours.

Jim Auld, then a twenty-year-old dental technician, was arrested on his return from a party; when he opened his front door, he saw a paratrooper pointing a rifle at him. 'I was very apprehensive about that situation—being taken away in the middle of the night—and at that stage I said to my mother, "Look, you can see that I am not marked in any way. This is the guy who is in charge, so if there are any marks on me later, this is the guy that you need to remember."'

Auld was taken to Girdwood Barracks, one of the registration points for internees. He spent part of the day in Crumlin Road Jail, and then he was handed back to the military.

'They took me into a small room where I was made to lie on

a camp bed and they just started beating me. They were screaming at me, "Keep your hands at your sides! Keep your hands at your sides!" Then every time I tried to keep my hands at my sides they were whacking me. They kicked the shit out of me. And eventually when I woke up again I was lying on the camp bed and one of the soldiers who had been beating me gave me a cigarette and he lit it and he said, "Here, you poor bastard, you're going to need that." And it was the first indication I had that there was something serious going to happen.'

A hood was placed over Auld's head; he was handcuffed and then, with a group of other men, led to a helicopter. 'As soon as the helicopter landed, we were kicked out. Someone grabbed me and I was dragged along, with the hood on, couldn't see where I was going at all, and they just ran me straight into a post. Straight into my head, flying full force into it, and I just went down. I was dragged inside and stripped and made to put on a boiler suit. Then they brought me into this room and put me against the wall, spread-eagled, my hands way above my head. There was a hissing sound in the background, at that stage I thought it was a pipe hissing.'

Auld and the other men were about to undergo a combination of tortures. The hood was meant to contribute to his sense of isolation. The noise increased in intensity (other men described it as the sound of an airplane engine) and for the next week it never stopped. Many of the men now recall it as the worst part of the ordeal. The men were also deprived of food and water and were not allowed to sleep (Auld was kept awake for six days). The spread-eagled position was part of the torture: Auld was forced to stand about a yard from the wall he was leaning against so that most of his weight rested on his hands, a position which produces enormous strain; some of the men were afterwards unable to hold a mug or write. Most of them were also denied access to a toilet and had to urinate and defecate in their boiler suits.

The combination of tortures—hooding, noise bombardment, food deprivation, sleep deprivation and the painful spread-eagled position—later came to be known as 'the five techniques'. Their effects were extreme. Paddy Joe McClean, a schoolteacher from County Tyrone, heard a firing-squad and saw his own funeral.

Patrick Shivers, a civil rights activist from Toomebridge, saw a table covered with glasses of fizzing lemonade; he began praying to his dead son, and the child appeared to him. Francis McGuigan, an active Republican from Belfast, imagined he was in the company of friends and couldn't understand why they wouldn't take off his handcuffs. At one stage his interrogators asked him to spell his name. He couldn't. They were amused. They then asked him to count to ten. He refused: he was afraid he wouldn't be able to do it.

'I didn't know what was going on, where I was or who was doing what to me,' Auld recalls. 'And your hands up against the wall, after ten or fifteen minutes, they start getting numb, so I dropped them down to my sides, anu as soon as I did, I got beaten with the batons, just beaten solid. And my hands were forced back up to the wall. And very quickly you got the message that you weren't supposed to move your hands. So I tried to show them I was willingly standing against the wall, I only wanted to start the circulation again in my arms, so I brought one hand down, but I was immediately set on again. But you can only stay like that for so long, and again my hands just dropped down. And again, set on and knocked unconscious. And I woke up and they threw me back up again. It just went on like that. I know that I wet myself. It seemed to go on for days.

'The noise started getting to me. At one stage it was a noise at the far corner of the room, and now, at this stage it was beside me. I was getting more and more confused. Every time I fell down they just kicked me all around the place and forced me back up on to the wall. I was eventually brought into a room where they pulled my hood up. There was a plain-clothes guy there and he started asking me questions about the IRA—did I know anybody in the IRA and that. And I was desperate and I said, Yes, I know everybody. Who did you want? Joe Cahill? Sean MacStiofain? They were the names that anybody knew. They immediately pulled my hood down again and beat me, dragged me out and forced me back up on to the wall. And they just beat me.

'After about four days they set me on the ground and lifted the hood up to my nose and they gave me a piece of bread and a cup of water. And I was afraid to take the bread in case they took the water away. Because my mouth was dry, completely dry. And I was afraid—I needed the water, I needed the fluid—and I was afraid to take the bread, so I threw the bread away and I took the water. And someone lifted the bread up and he gave it back to me again and he stuck a bit of it in my mouth. And he held the cup up and gave me one drink of it and then took the whole lot away. They pulled the hood down again and there was obviously two or three of them. As one of them took the bread off me, another couple of them threw me back up on the wall. And one of them punched me in the kidneys because I can remember it knocked all the wind out of me. I went straight down and they all seemed to be in a circle around me, beating me.

'And I remember crying at that stage and saying, "I just can't take this, Mister, I'm sorry, I just don't know what to do." And I couldn't do anything, and I felt so helpless and so isolated that I would have told anybody anything. The interrogations were nothing for me because I wasn't in the position to tell them what they wanted to know. I admitted to being in everything but the crib with the baby Jesus, and if they had asked me about that I would have said, "Yes, the crib as well, I'm in the background of it there," because I was so frightened of what they were doing to me. I would love to see the records of it, to see what I did tell them, because it couldn't be anything but funny, because it is all lies and desperation. But when it was happening, it wasn't funny.

'All I could think was that these people had done so many bad things to me that they could never let me out alive to tell people. Because it would destroy them. And then I thought, the logical thing is for them to kill me and say that I got killed in a shooting or something. And that was what was in my head, that they were going to kill me.'

Auld knows he was missing for nine days. He believes that on the eighth day he was taken off the wall and into a room with a mattress in it. 'I was that frightened that it didn't enter my head to take the hood off. I was just that petrified. And eventually a Branchman, a plain-clothes man came in, and he said, "You should have just taken off the hood." And he brought me in something to eat, it was like watery stew. And because I couldn't hold it—my hands were useless—he fed me. He gave me a Mars Bar, he gave me a Coke, he gave me three or four different meals that day. And he was continually talking to me about just everyday things. And he told me that it was over, I wouldn't be going back to the wall, I wouldn't be getting touched again, that he didn't want anything to happen to me. And at that stage, I thought he was God. I thought he was the nicest human being alive. He was my friend.

'He told me exactly what was going to happen. We would be going back in the helicopter and landing in the Crumlin Road Jail. And when I got out I wasn't to look back at the helicopter. I would be set on the edge when the helicopter landed and I was just to slide off and walk to the screws who would be waiting for me. And then he put my hood back on and he made sure that it wasn't too tight, that I had plenty of air, and he was very civil about it. And we got into the helicopter.

'We were gone about twenty minutes. When the helicopter landed, I sat down and there was an arm on my back and it pushed me off, and as that happened, another hand came and pulled the hood off my head, and I was pushed forwards towards the two screws.

'And I think it was the first realization for me how serious things were, because the look that I saw on the screws' faces was one of sheer horror at my appearance. They were absolutely horrified. And they grabbed me and helped me into a mini-bus and brought me around to Crumlin Road Jail. They fed me sweets and were running in and out of the cell for three quarters of an hour, asking me did I want anything, giving me a packet of cigarettes, giving me a box of matches, and continually asking me did I want coffee or tea, until I was moved to D Wing, the basement, the holding cells. I was there overnight, and while I was there, other guys, whose voices I recognized, started talking and I got up and I was talking through the bars with them, and I realized then that there were other people who had gone through the same process.'

The story of what happened to the men slowly leaked out to the newspapers. Edward Heath appointed a Commission, headed by Sir Edmund Compton, to investigate the charges. Compton concluded that no torture had occurred. The five techniques, he said, were 'ill-treatment' but not brutality, as the term 'brutality' implied that the perpetrators had enjoyed or been indifferent to the victims' pain, and there was no indication that this had been the case.

In the Commons debate that followed, Home Secretary Reginald Maulding said, 'There was no permanent injury whatever, physical or mental, to any of the men concerned.' Lord Carrington told television reporters that the men who had been subjected to the techniques were 'thugs and murderers', a seemingly defamatory comment given that none of the men had been charged with any crime after what the government claimed was such effective interrogation.

T he victims were held in Crumlin Road Jail for a few weeks, and then moved to the main internment camp at Long Kesh.

Sean McKenna, at forty-two the oldest of the fourteen men who were tortured, seems to have had the worst reaction. At one point he had been unable to remember his name or the names of his children. Jim Auld, who shared a cell with McKenna at the Crumlin Road Jail, recalls that the older man's hair turned white and that he wept continually. Other ex-internees recall that McKenna became convinced that he was receiving secret messages over the television, and that he believed other inmates were plotting against him. In May 1972, the *Guardian* reported that McKenna shook continually, found it hard to articulate sentences, suffered from severe headaches and had recurring nightmares about being attacked by groups of men.

McKenna was released three years after his arrest. A psychiatrist who examined him shortly afterwards found him to be displaying 'gross symptoms of anxiety'. A few months later, on 5 June 1975, Sean McKenna died of a heart attack. He was forty-five.

Pat Shivers, a civil rights activist from Toomebridge, was the second oldest of the victims. Auld recalls that Shivers 'couldn't control his facial expression, his head shook and his eyelids were twitching.' Shivers was released after only three months of internment. In a recent interview, his wife recalled that after his release he panicked every time he saw a soldier or a policeman; that he suffered from nightmares; and that he sometimes gasped for air, as if he could not get enough. His former cellmate at the Crumlin Road Jail said that he had woken up one night to see Shivers standing against the wall in the torture position. Shivers died of stomach cancer in 1985. He was fifty-four.

Michael Montgomery was a member of the IRA at the time of his arrest. After his release, his wife Doris recalled, 'He never slept. He twisted, turned, shouted, bawled at night. I was scared of him. He used to put a gun to my head and threaten to shoot me.' She left her husband in 1977. Michael Montgomery died of a heart attack on 1 December 1984. He was forty-nine.

Liam Shannon developed chronic diarrhoea after his interrogation and in 1975 was found to have Chrone's disease. Gerard McKerr, who was one of the strongest of the men arrested, was diagnosed as having cancer of the lymph glands shortly after his release from Long Kesh in 1974. Another survivor, arrested in the Republic of Ireland on charges that were later dropped, had a flashback upon being placed in a cell; he believed he was in the custody of the Royal Ulster Constabulary and barricaded himself in. A psychiatrist was able to get him out only by having the guards change into civilian clothes.

Recognizing that the Compton Commission's report had raised the question of what limits should be placed on the security forces in Northern Ireland, Reginald Maulding announced the formation of a second committee that would consider 'authorized procedures for the interrogation of prisoners suspected of terrorism.' The appointed committee consisted of Lord Parker, who served as chairman, Lord Gardiner, and Mr J. A. Boyd-Carpenter. They met in secret and heard no evidence from detainees.

The three men came to two different conclusions. In his minority report, Lord Gardiner revealed that the five techniques were taught at an army intelligence centre in England; that instructors from the centre had given a seminar on the techniques to the Royal Ulster Constabulary in April 1971; and that officers from the centre had been present when the techniques were used in Northern Ireland that August. Based on the medical evidence he had collected, Gardiner characterized the five techniques as the induction of 'an artificial psychosis or episode of insanity', and he predicted that the induced condition would become permanent. He went on to point out that there was nothing in domestic law which allowed a soldier or policeman to do what had been done, and that what had been done was therefore a crime.

The majority report, prepared by Lord Parker and Boyd-Carpenter, concluded that there was no reason 'to rule out these techniques on moral grounds' and that any mental disorientation could be 'expected to disappear within a matter of hours at the end of the interrogation.' The two men also suggested that one of the advantages of this method of interrogation was that it had the potential to establish the innocence of the detainee.

The Irish government took up the men's cases, filing a complaint on their behalf with the European Commission on Human Rights.

The British government refused to allow the Commission to visit the scenes where the abuse had taken place. It denied the Commission access to interrogation records and instructed the policemen and soldiers who testified not to answer questions about the five techniques. The government also refused to allow the Commission to question the officials who had ordered the use of the techniques; instead civil servants were sent who read statements and refused to be cross-examined. In its defence, the government said that the techniques had been very useful in gathering intelligence during British campaigns in Palestine, Malaya, Kenya, Cyprus, the British Cameroons, British Guyana, Brunei, Aden, Borneo and the Persian Gulf.

On 25 January 1976, the Commission ruled unanimously that the use of the techniques amounted to torture and inhuman and degrading treatment.

The *Daily Telegraph* said the Commission was wrong. The *Daily Express* said that no serious physical or mental injury had been inflicted, and that it must be understood that the security forces were not dealing with normally law-abiding citizens, but with fanatics. The *Guardian* suggested that if the government of Ireland took the case on to the European Court of Human Rights, as it was threatening to do, it would be 'force-feeding the Provisionals propaganda.'

The Irish government did take the case to the European Court of Human Rights, partly because Ireland wanted Britain to prosecute those responsible. At that point, Britain stopped contesting that the five techniques amounted to torture; the government declared that 'no beneficial interest would be served' in contesting that particular finding. There was speculation that the government was trying to avoid having to produce the police, soldiers and politicians who were responsible. The British government pledged that the techniques would never again be used and pointed out that the victims had been compensated (an average of fourteen thousand pounds had been paid to each of the fourteen men); the court was urged to conclude that no further action was necessary.

On 18 January 1978, the European Court, by a vote of thirteen to four, ruled that the five techniques were inhuman and degrading treatment, but not torture. 'They did not occasion suffering of the particular intensity and cruelty implied by the word "torture" as so understood,' said the court. The majority seemed to agree with the position of Sir Gerald Fitzmaurice, the British judge on the court, who argued that if having one's fingernail torn out, or being impaled on a stake through the rectum, or being roasted on an electric grid is torture, then the five techniques was something less. (Fitzmaurice believed that the techniques did not constitute inhuman and degrading treatment either, but he alone held that view.)

The judges did not order that anyone should be prosecuted. They argued that they did not have the power to order a state to institute criminal or disciplinary proceedings in accordance with its domestic law.

The *Daily Telegraph* called the ruling 'a triumph'. The newspaper admitted that Britain had been found to employ inhuman and degrading methods in its treatment of suspects who had not been charged with any crime. But, it asked, 'Can a state threatened by anarchy be properly and realistically expected not

John Conroy

to employ such methods?'
Amnesty International said that despite the judges' decision, it still considered the five techniques to be torture.

Jim Auld was among the men who suffered severe after-effects. In May 1972 the press reported that he had collapsed in his hut at the Long Kesh internment camp and had been taken to hospital, and that he was having black-outs, violent headaches, insomnia and nightmares. Three weeks later he was released to a mental hospital in Armagh in the company of a psychiatrist. When he found out that he was not legally compelled to be there, he walked out.

His black-outs continued over the next two years, occurring as frequently as four or five times a week. He found it impossible to keep a job; over the course of the next two years he worked as a bricklayer, a barman, a driver and a labourer. He felt that he could not explain what he had been through, and that even if he could, no one would understand.

He still stuffers from the effects of the five techniques. He says that he has lost the ability to spell, and that he can read for only a short period of time before he loses concentration. He is easily startled, and has recurring nightmares, particularly when he talks about the torture. After our first meeting, the dreams returned.

I met him again last summer as the twentieth anniversary of his ordeal approached, and after our interview, he gave another to a Belfast journalist who was preparing a retrospective piece about internment. Within days Auld had come down with shingles and high blood pressure. He spent the anniversary bed-ridden and in considerable pain.

The case of Jim Auld and his fellow victims has no end. Torture's aftermath has a well established pattern: the perpetrators, well known to the government, are never charged. The men who gave the orders are never named. The politicians who sanctioned the treatment are never called to account.

In Northern Ireland, that pattern is now a twenty-year-old

tradition. Last November, Amnesty International reported that between 1988 and 1990, 683 people arrested under Northern Ireland's emergency legislation complained that they had been assaulted while in custody, but not a single member of the security forces was disciplined or prosecuted as a result. The government has often paid compensation to victims of assault and torture, but those payments are made in out-of-court settlements which require no admission of responsibility.

Last September, the Northern Irish police arrested Brian Shivers, a twenty-year-old Catholic from Toomebridge who has cystic fibrosis and asthma. Shivers was deprived of his inhaler and forced to stand with his hands above his head for a long period of time. Suddenly he collapsed. He says he was subsequently hit in the genitals, grabbed by the throat, beaten about the head and deprived of food. He was not permitted to see a doctor. After his release, he was hospitalized for a week. He is the son of Pat Shivers, the civil rights activist who was hooded and tortured with Jim Auld, and who died in 1985.

JOHN BERGER

INTO THEIR LABOURS

John Berger's epic trilogy of rural Europe, comprising
PIG EARTH, ONCE IN EUROPA and LILAC AND
FLAG, published in one volume for the first time.

GRANTA BOOKS

PEREGRINE HODSON
THE DOLPHIN OF AMBLE

A friend of mine met Freddy during the summer. The meeting lasted less than half an hour but it affected her deeply. She told me about swimming with a dolphin in the sea off the north coast of England. The dolphin's name was Freddy. She gave me the number of the lifeboat mechanic who took her in his boat to meet the dolphin. I thought of telephoning the man to arrange a meeting, but for some reason I didn't get around to it.

Some months later I was reading a newspaper when I noticed an article about an animal rights activist prosecuted for an act of indecency with a dolphin. The man was accused of 'committing a lewd, obscene and disgusting act and outraging public decency by behaving in an indecent manner with a bottle-nosed dolphin to the great disgust and annoyance of divers of Her Majesty's subjects within whose purview the act was committed.' The dolphin was called Freddy. I tried telephoning the man with the boat but there was no reply. The trial ended in an acquittal. The dolphin was still at large. I decided to go to Amble.

I started north one morning before sunrise with a friend called Simon. We arrived in Amble at midday and parked the car by the community centre. The walls were scrawled with graffiti: *Angela is a dog. Fuck. Biff and Munch. Paul is a Lush.* On the way to the waterfront we passed Johnny's Bingo and Social Club. The sign in front read, 'Open 6.30–10.00 p.m. daily. KEEP CLEAR.'

We were the only people on the waterfront. Seagulls cried over the sound of mast lines tapping in the wind. We were cold and hungry and went into the first pub we could find. The room had a low ceiling. A group of men stood at one end of the bar and a big man worked the beer pumps.

We ordered beers and the man offered us a choice of sandwiches: cheese and tomato, cheese and onion, or corned beef—'Beef in a tin,' the big man said. 'Corned beef. You'll enjoy it.' He tore two squares from a roll of paper towel, put them in front of us, and placed our sandwiches—one cheese and onion and one corned beef—on the squares. He made little grunts as he moved. He smiled and asked if we'd come to see the dolphin. 'It's the fifth largest tourist attraction in this part of England,' he said. 'I forget the others. But it's the fifth.'

Photo: Simon Westcott

Dunstan had Dunstanborough Castle; Howick had Howick Gardens; Amble had the Dolphin.

'With the mines closing and the fishing industry dying it's not easy. Twenty per cent unemployed, maybe more. Nobody knows with all the retraining schemes these days. But the dolphin makes a difference. Apart from the pie factory the only work is painting and decorating, or the tourist trade. The dolphin's been a big tourist attraction.' We ordered more sandwiches and asked where we could stay for the night. The big man said there were rooms in a guest-house near the harbour. The people there knew the operator of the boat which would take us to the dolphin.

As we put on our coats he wished us a good time with the dolphin and someone called out to us, 'Don't do anything I wouldn't do,' and they all laughed and one said, 'You'd do anything.'

The windows had net curtains and there was a sign saying VACANCIES over three photographs of dolphins. Mrs Henderson greeted us. She was a large middle-aged woman wearing a T-shirt with the words, 'Freddy, the friendliest dolphin'. The rate was eleven pounds a person for bed and breakfast. She had a kind face but seemed nervous. She asked if we were vegetarians. We said we were happy with anything.

'Some of them aren't,' she said, her face relaxing. 'I put a plate of bacon and eggs in front of one of them and he went Aaargh! I told him I'm not a mind-reader. But that's what some of them do when they see it. Aaargh! Not just meat. I've even had some of them do it with kippers. That's why I always ask them, just in case. Make yourselves at home anyway.'

The television room was at the end of the hall. The bedroom was up the stairs and to the left and was unlocked. If we wanted anything we had to knock on a glass door marked PRIVATE. Mrs Henderson said there would be a pot of tea for us in the television room when we came back from the dolphin.

The bedroom had two beds, a wash basin, a chair and a cupboard. There was a picture of a rose on one wall. The window looked over the car-park and the harbour, up the river to the castle in the distance.

At the harbour we waited to meet Gordon Easton, who operated the boat. I read an information sheet distributed by International Dolphin Watch on the Amble Dolphin.

On 25 September, Freddy the dolphin, who has stayed in the mouth of the river Coquet at Amble for the past three years, was struck by a propeller and suffered eleven lacerations on his right flank . . . In order to give the cuts the best opportunity to seal and obviate opening of the wounds by accidental contact with fins etc. it was requested that swimmers should stay clear of the dolphin, and notices to this effect were posted in Amble . . . On a visit to Amble on 7 and 8 October I was able personally to observe Freddy and swim with him. From these interactions I gained the distinct impression that Freddy was missing the level of contact he normally enjoyed and was deliberately seeking human company. Indeed, while I watched him from a boat, Freddy swam away, caught a fish, tossed it in the air and played with it vigorously before consuming it and returning to me.

I looked at the bottom of the page. It was signed: 'Doctor Horace E. Dobbs'. I read on.

Gordon Easton, the mechanic of the lifeboat, has spent more hours at close quarters with Freddy than anyone else. He has agreed to act as our Dolphin Ambassador in Amble. As such he is happy to take visitors out in his boat and advise them how to behave in the water in the presence of the dolphin.

I wondered what Gordon Easton, lifeboat mechanic, on call night and day to rescue people from the waters of the North Sea, thought about being appointed Dolphin Ambassador, and what he thought of Doctor Horace E. Dobbs.

A man with tousled reddish-blond hair came towards us along the jetty. We introduced ourselves and Gordon Easton said we'd come at the right time: the tide was out and the sea calm. I was asking if the dolphin was about, when I saw, over Gordon's shoulder, beyond the pier, a movement like a wave, only different,

231

on the surface of the sea. 'That's him,' said Gordon. 'That's where he likes to be.'

I got into the boat and put on a dry suit over my jeans and sweater. Gordon's dog chewed at the arms while I tried to find the legs. I pushed my head up through the neck and Simon zipped me across the chest. Gordon turned down the motor.

'Wave your arm if you're in trouble,' he said. 'You don't want water leaking in. The cold creeps over you. Don't leave it too late.'

I pressed some air out through the valve over my chest and put a leg over the side of the boat. Simon told me to look happy and I lowered myself into the water.

I floated without any effort. The spray from the waves blew in my face and my hands were freezing. The rest of my body was warm.

Gordon's dog became excited. He looked over the side of the boat, wagging his tail and barking. Gordon had said that the dog would know when the dolphin was near. I was wondering if I would have an intuition or feel an underwater vibration passing through my body, when there was a gush and a hiss behind me and a smell of fish and a splash. I knew the smell—fish eaters' breath. The hairs on the back of my neck were rising, and I felt like a clumsy star of arms and legs above the dolphin.

A touch on my right hand, then a few seconds later, on my left. He knew exactly where his body was in the water—he was under the surface moving past my right hand again, just touching, caressing. He did the same with my left. It was like a greeting; it had pattern and symmetry.

I was some distance from the boat. The dry suit supported me. The dolphin had vanished. Perhaps he'd checked me out with his sonar, and the meeting was over. I swam towards the boat. Then I felt something tapping the soles of my feet and saw air bubbles rising in a plume and breaking the surface around me.

I got closer to the boat. Gordon asked if I was OK and I said yes. I imagined the dolphin chasing fishes under my feet. Suddenly he broke the surface just beside me in a glistening arc of silver-grey flesh set with a great eye, and as he rolled over I rested my hand on his body and felt where the propeller had cut him: a dozen or so straight ridges of scar tissue at regular, machine-made intervals.

My hands were freezing; an icy sensation worked down my back and around my waist. I worried about a leak in the suit. The dolphin reappeared, this time almost head on, and I stroked him like Gordon told me, under the neck which was soft as a silk stocking underwater, and as he dived I felt the end of his fin at the tips of my fingers.

It wasn't easy getting into the boat. Simon helped me on to the deck. The sleeve of the dry suit had trapped part of my sweater. I pulled back the rubber cuff and water poured out as if I'd turned on a tap. Gordon laughed and asked if I was warm enough.

On the way back Gordon told me about the people who came to swim with the dolphin. 'You get all types. Mystical ones,' he grinned. 'They come from all over the world—Germans, Swedes, Hawaiians. Some of them are surprised by how we live. We're poor. There's a lot of poverty.' The way he said the word 'poverty', as a farmer might speak about a drought, or a fisherman describe a season of empty nets, made it sound like a natural misfortune. I thought of the shops selling bric-à-brac in the high street, with names like Nostalgia and Memories.

I asked about the dolphin's scars. Gordon explained how the accident happened. A member of the Royal family was visiting the lifeboat station. A lady-in-waiting wanted to see Freddy and a police launch was commandeered. Freddy was used to boats with single propellers. The twin propellers of the police launch confused him. He misjudged a turn and a propeller caught him along his right flank. The cuts were six inches deep. 'It was a miracle he wasn't killed. But he just carried on as normal. He still likes coming up behind boats and getting close to the propellers.'

Back at the guest-house I stripped off my wet clothes and had a hot bath. Then I joined Simon in the television room. He was reading the visitors' book.

A gas fire was burning. On the television was a collecting box for the Royal National Lifeboat Institution. The receipts for the

233

past eighteen months were carefully displayed. Over the fire and by the door were pictures of lifeboats; two framed photographs of a helicopter rescue hung above the television. The other pictures were of dolphins: looming out of a watery darkness like a white shadow, silhouetted against the sun-freckled surface of the sea, a smiling prodigy.

There was a knock at the door and Mrs Henderson appeared. She didn't come right into the room but stayed by the door.

'Did you get the touch?' she said.

I described what happened.

'You were lucky,' she said. 'He's got you first time ever. Not everyone gets the touch.' I asked if she had had it. She closed the door and sat on an arm of the sofa.

'I shouldn't have been in the sea. It was really choppy. I didn't think I was going to get it. My first touch—I was standing on him. Marvellous! I thought, I'm on solid ground. He was underneath my feet. But my husband's never seen Freddy. He doesn't like water. He almost drowned when he was a child. You won't get him into a boat.'

Simon asked how the dolphin came to Amble, and she told of the first sighting by the men at the lighthouse, three years before. At first they thought it was a shark. Then someone from the Dolphinarium at Flamingoland confirmed it was a dolphin. 'Gradually he got closer to people. They thought he'd come here to die, he was so thin. But now he's big and strong. He's found a good feeding spot at the mouth of the river—the salmon sense fresh water and they swim towards it. Freddy waits for them between the pier and the headland. A few fishermen complain, but we're all fond of him. No locals have gone overboard—if you know what I mean, no nutters. It's not like the dolphin at Dingle in Ireland. There's no racket here.'

Simon asked who the 'nutters' were.

'I'd prefer not to talk about it,' she said. 'The court case and everything. There's a lot of feelings, if you know what I mean.' There was an awkward silence. Simon said how much he'd enjoyed reading the visitors' book. Mrs Henderson smiled.

'We've had some lovely people here,' she said. 'All sorts. Ones with emotional problems who come for healing. We had youngsters here who were involved in the Hillsborough disaster. Angie was one of identical twins—a car killed her sister, she was lost without her. But when she'd been swimming with Freddy she realized there were other things in life. Nicola was a kidney transplant girl—a little spelk of a girl. Freddy helped her.'

I asked Mrs Henderson how old Freddy was. She arranged a cushion on the sofa. 'He won't be here for ever. One day a mine will go off. The new-fangled nets go deep and sometimes they pick up mines. Someone caught one in his fishing net. The mine disposal lads came to stay here. I did some sarnies for them. I was afraid that Freddy would follow their boat. They wanted to keep Freddy behind the pier, but he went near the mine. I couldn't watch. I was trying to tidy up in here with a friend. We heard it blow. She said, "I'll go and see." But he was fine. Fifteen of us sat in the kitchen celebrating with the lads. It was this time of year, before Christmas. I went down to Newcastle and I've never enjoyed shopping so much. Anyway,' she stood up, 'it's time I was feeding the dog.'

When she had left I opened the visitors' book and read.

Cliff and Gladys from Darlington: comfortable friendly stay. Exciting dolphin watch.

Kutira from the Kahlua Hawaiian Institute: an outstanding experience to swim belly to belly with Freddy —Kealoha (love) his new Hawaiian name. To undulate and feel the loving touch and wisdom of this beautiful friend. Also don't miss Gordon the Keeper of the Dolphin-Wisdom. He is truly a guide into the Dreamtime.

Steve: gob-smacked!

Maria: back again. I need to visit Freddy and Amble. Shame about the wild sea, only got in once, but it was enough for my baby (to be). Twelve weeks into pregnancy to say 'hello' to Freddy. I will be back when I've had the baby to introduce them properly. Special thanks to all who make us feel so welcome. It's home from home.

In the morning, after breakfast, Simon called his girl-friend and I changed into the dry suit in the television room. It was easier without Gordon's dog chewing everything. We stepped outside and the air was cold. The snow in the shadows was the colour of the sky; the snow in the sunshine was whiter than the back of a Christmas card.

Gordon was waiting for us. We climbed into the boat. There was ice on the ropes and snow on the deck. 'Beautiful morning,' Gordon said, 'not too cold. When it's very cold, the ropes are frozen solid. You have to piss on the ropes to untie them.'

The dolphin joined us at the mouth of the harbour.

'He heard the boat's engine,' said Gordon. 'He knew it meant visitors.'

Once again the dolphin presented his body to my hand, slid by my fingers and turned over with a lazy splash. The white flesh of his belly felt as smooth as melting ice. The scars passed under my fingers. For a moment his eye looked, or seemed to look, into my own. Then he rolled over and his tail was in the air and and he was gone.

'That's how he says goodbye,' said Gordon. 'He's busy feeding now. He won't come back till he's finished.'

We shook hands and I said we hoped to come again. 'Let's hope Freddy's here as well,' said Gordon. Then we loaded our things into the car, said goodbye to Mrs Henderson and drove south.

VICTORIA TOKAREVA
HAPPY ENDING

I died at daybreak, between four and five.
My hands and feet were cold, as though someone had pulled gloves and wet stockings on them. The cold reached my heart, and my heart stopped. I felt like I'd sunk to the bottom of a well. I'd never been to the bottom of a well, but then, I'd never been dead either. My face stretched into a mask that I couldn't control. Nothing hurt.

At eight o'clock I heard the shuffle of footsteps in the hall. It was Yuranya, my son, coming out of the nursery. Barefoot, I thought. He always walked barefoot, like a half-wild forest boy, and I always said, 'Feet, Yuranya.' He shuffled down the hall and stopped near his father's room. My husband coughed and turned over. The door squeaked—Yuranya must have pushed it open —and he asked in an ingratiating whisper: 'Are you up?'

'What do you want?' my husband responded in a touchy voice. He hated being bothered at the weekend.

Yuranya hissed in the same whisper, 'I have to go to the cinema at nine o'clock.' He seemed to think that by whispering he wouldn't wake his father, who might have a conversation with him in his sleep.

'Wake Mama up,' my husband ordered. He didn't like taking on other people's responsibilities. He also regarded his own with distaste.

The door to my room squeaked. Yuranya stood there silently, then said: 'She's asleep.'

'She'll get up,' said my husband.

'She's asleep,' repeated Yuranya, 'and very pale.'

At twelve o'clock they took me to the hospital. The next day they brought me back and put me in a dress which someone had purchased for me in Paris a year ago. It had hung in the wardrobe since then.

My sixth-floor neighbour said: 'They won't accept her in the other world. She's too young.'

'She left her little boy,' sighed another neighbour. She had seen her son through to his pension; I hadn't seen mine through primary school. She shook her head in contemplating what I had missed.

Yuranya moved about proudly. Everyone petted him; he was

flattered by the attention. I had warned him: 'If I'm not around and everyone says I've died, don't believe them.'

'Where will you be?'

'I'll settle on a cloud and watch over you.'

'All right,' Yuranya agreed.

My husband never believed my illnesses were real, and now he didn't believe my death. He thought it was another one of my tricks.

The flat was full of people. I had thought that fewer would come, that there wouldn't be anyone to bury me. I usually do things myself. If I could have buried myself, I would have. But they managed without me. They arranged a cemetery plot and completed the paperwork.

An official from the registry bureau, a woman in a grey sweater, gave my husband a receipt and demanded my passport. My husband handed her the passport; she glanced at it without interest, tore it in half and threw it in a wicker rubbish basket. At that moment my husband understood that I had been dismissed from life and could not be recalled. He was free now, but he didn't know what to do. I had been more useful than inconvenient. He looked sluggish, as if he also had taken sleeping pills.

My girl-friends Alya and Elya rushed over on their lunch break. Both were pretty—but I alone saw Alya's beauty, while no one missed Elya's. Alya lived alone, without love or a family. She had thought of me as successful and didn't understand. Elya was as successful as I and as tired of options. Ravished by them, emptied. She too had a dress from Paris hanging in her wardrobe. But now she knew: she'd never end her own life; she'd drink the cup to the bottom.

They gazed, depressed and silent, at my mask-face. 'We're all guilty,' said Alya. 'No one wanted to know. No one wanted to help.'

'How could we help, when she didn't need anyone?'

The phone rang often. My husband answered and said that I couldn't come and speak because I was dead. But did He call? Probably not. He was waiting for me to call. He and I had decided: love was no reason to destroy our children's lives.

'Let's split up,' I proposed.

'But how will we live?' he asked.

I didn't know. 'Well, let's go on this way,' I said at last.

'This is no way to live.'

'What's the answer then?'

'The happiest ending would be for me to die in an airplane crash.'

'What about your children?' I asked.

'They would love me in memory.'

Did he call? Or will he in a couple of days?

'She died,' my husband will say.

He won't say anything. Neither will my husband. Then my husband will say goodbye and hang up.

Death is boring. It offers no options.

In the evening my mother arrived. She told my husband that she wouldn't leave him anything. She'd rather smash every plate and rip every pillowcase.

He got mad. 'Stop talking nonsense,' he said.

Mama replied that my death was his fault and it would have been better if he'd died, not me.

My husband said, well, that was *her* point of view. From *his* mother's point of view, things were better this way.

Around ten o'clock everyone left. High above me a clock ticked. There was a noise like a tap turned on at full force. I guessed that my husband was watching soccer on the television.

My mother walked in and asked, 'What are you doing, watching soccer?'

He replied: 'What else am I supposed to do?'

They buried me two days later.

The snow was thin on the ground; streams were running. The earth was moist and heavy and was a dispiriting influence on the living.

There were fresh graves nearby, decorated with artificial wreaths and covered with cellophane. The rain and mud would pass and the cellophane would be removed.

The earth knocked against my coffin. The mound was small, barely detectable. They had strewn it with flowers.

I saw God. He was young and handsome. I went up to Him in my long, shiny dress and looked into His eyes.

'Forgive me,' I said.

'People are always asking me to leave them on earth longer, and you left early. Why?'

'I didn't see a way out.'

'Is this a way out?'

'There aren't options here. I'm tired of options.'

'You couldn't be patient?'

'I couldn't.'

Something reached me from my former existence, and I burst into tears.

He stroked my hair: 'Don't cry, I pity you.'

'I called on you—I was waiting for you to intervene. Why didn't you hear me?'

'I heard you. I said: be patient, all will pass.'

'Why didn't I hear you?'

'Because Love was stronger in you than God. You heard Love.'

God passed a palm over my cheek, wiping away the tears. He was tall, long-haired and looked like a contemporary youth. Only his eyes were different.

'What do you want?' asked God.

'I want to see him.'

God led me along the Milky Way. Then He stopped, waved His hand and released my soul. My soul flew in darkness for a long time, then plunged into light. It circled over his home and flew in the open window. It rested on the window sill. He was sitting at the table and playing cards with his daughter. My soul went up to him carefully and looked at his cards. He had lost. I couldn't let him know.

He called two days later, as usual. I picked up the receiver. He didn't say anything. But I knew it was him. I said: 'I'll die, and you'll lose your life.'

'What do you mean, you'll die?' he said. 'You're only saying that.'

We were silent. We could go on like that, silent, for a long time and not get bored. We stood at opposite ends of the city and listened to one another's breathing.

Translated from the Russian by Jamey Gambrell

241

NEW FROM GRANTA BOOKS

MONKFISH MOON
ROMESH GUNESEKERA

The nine haunting stories in this book announce an extraordinary writing talent.

Gunesekera reveals lives shaped by the luxuriant tropical surroundings of Sri Lanka and disoriented by resurgent violence.

This is a paradise in which the sudden presence of silence in a city brings fear, where civil war invades a marriage thousands of miles away, and where one night a young girl goes dancing and a man discovers his life is ending ...

GRANTA BOOKS

SALMAN RUSHDIE
AT THE AUCTION OF THE
RUBY SLIPPERS

The bidders who have assembled for the auction of the magic slippers bear little resemblance to your usual saleroom crowd. The Auctioneers have publicized the event widely and are prepared for all comers. People venture out but rarely nowadays; nevertheless, and rightly, the Auctioneers believed this prize would tempt us from our bunkers. High feelings are anticipated, and accordingly, in addition to the standard facilities provided for the comfort and security of the more notable personages, extra-large bronze cuspidors have been placed in the toilets, for the use of the physically sick, and psychiatrists of differing disciplines have been installed in strategically located neo-Gothic confessional booths, to counsel the sick at heart.

Most of us nowadays are sick.

There are no priests; the Auctioneers have drawn a line. The priests remain in other, nearby buildings, buildings with which they are familiar, hoping to deal with any psychic fall-out, any insanity overspill.

Units of obstetricians and helmeted police SWAT teams wait out of sight in side alleys in case the excitement leads to unexpected births or deaths. Lists of next of kin have been drawn up and their contact numbers recorded. A supply of strait-jackets has been laid in.

See: behind bullet-proof glass, the ruby slippers sparkle. Movie stars are here, among the bidders, bringing their glossy, spangled auras to the saleroom. When one of us collides with a star's priceless (and fragile) aura, he or she is instantly knocked to the floor by a security team and hustled out to the waiting paddy-wagons. Such incidents slightly reduce the crush in the Grand Saleroom.

The memorabilia junkies are out in predictable force, and now with a ducking movement of the head one of them applies her desperate lips to the slippers' transparent cage, setting off the state-of-the-art alarm system whose programmers have neglected to teach it about the relative harmlessness of such an osculation. The alarm system pumps a hundred thousand volts of electricity into the silicon-implanted lips of the glass kisser, terminating her interest in the proceedings. It is an unpleasantly whiffy moment, but it fails to deter a second *aficionado* from the same suicidal kissery. When we learn that this crazed moron was the lover of the first fatality, we wonder rather at the mysteries of love, whilst reaching once again for our perfumed handkerchiefs.

A fancy-dress party is in full swing. Wizards, Lions, Scarecrows are in plentiful supply. They jostle crossly for position, stamping on one another's feet. There is a scarcity of Tin Men on account of the particular discomfort of the costume. Witches bide their time on the *balcons* and *gallerias* of the Grand Saleroom, living gargoyles with, in many cases, high credit ratings. One corner is occupied entirely by Totos, several of whom are copulating enthusiastically, obliging a rubber-gloved janitor to separate them so as to avoid giving public offence. He does this with no little delicacy and taste.

We, the public, are easily, lethally offended.

Around the—let us say—shrine of the ruby-sequinned slippers, pools of saliva have been forming. There are those of us who lack restraint, who drool. The jump-suited Latino janitor moves among us, a pail in one hand and a squeegee mop in the other. We admire and are grateful for his talent for self-effacement. He removes our mouth waters without causing any loss of face on our part.

Opportunities for encountering the miraculous are limited in our Nietzschean, relativistic universe. Behaviourist philosophers and quantum scientists crowd around the magic shoes.

Exiles, displaced persons of all sorts, even homeless tramps have turned up for a glimpse of the impossible, emerging from their subterranean hollows and braving the bazookas, the Uzi-armed gangs high on crack or ice, the smugglers, the emptiers of houses. The tramps wear stenchy jute ponchos and hawk noisily into the giant potted yuccas. They grab fistfuls of canapés from trays borne upon the superb palms of A-list caterers. Sushi is eaten by them with impressive quantities of *wasabi* sauce, to whose inflammatory powers the hoboes' innards seem impervious. SWAT teams are summoned and after a brief battle involving the use of rubber bullets and sedative darts the tramps are removed, clubbed into unconsciousness and driven away. They will be deposited some distance beyond the city limits, out there in that smoking no man's land into which we venture no more. Wild dogs will gather around them, eager for lunch. These are uncompromising times.

Political refugees are at the auction: conspirators, deposed monarchs, defeated factions, poets, bandit chieftains. Such figures no longer wear the black berets, pebble-lensed spectacles and enfolding greatcoats of yester-year, but strike resplendent attitudes in boxy silken jackets and high-waisted Japanese couture trousers. The women wear toreador jackets bearing sequinned representations of great works of art. One beauty parades *Guernica* on her back, while several others wear glittering scenes from the *Disasters of War* sequence by Francisco Goya. Incandescent in their suits of lights, the female political refugees fail to eclipse the ruby slippers, and huddle with their male comrades in small hissing bunches, periodically hurling imprecations, ink-pellets, spitballs and paper darts across the salon at rival clusters of *émigrés*. The guards at the exits crack their bullwhips idly and the politicals control themselves.

Disapproving critiques of the fetishizing of the slippers are offered by religious fundamentalists, who have been allowed to gain entry by virtue of the extreme liberalism of some of the Auctioneers, who argue that a civilized Saleroom must be a broad church, open, tolerant. The fundamentalists have expressed their desire to buy the magic footwear in order to burn it, and this is not, in the view of the liberal Auctioneers, an unreasonable request. What price tolerance if the intolerant are not tolerated also? Money insists on democracy; anyone's cash is as good as anyone else's. The fundamentalists fulminate from their soapboxes, and are ignored; but some senior figures present speak ominously of the thin end of the wedge.

Orphans arrive, hoping that the ruby slippers might transport them back through time as well as space, and reunite them with their deceased parents. There is even a baby in a perambulator; its nanny informs the Auctioneers of its desire to return to its preferred, unborn state, of its immense personal fortune, and of her legally certified powers of proxy voting. In the event of its unbirthing she will be its sole heir.

Men and women of dubious background are present —outlaws, untouchables, outcasts. The security forces deal

Salman Rushdie

brusquely with many of these.

'Home' has become a scattered, damaged, hydra-various concept in our present travails. There is so much to yearn for. There are so few rainbows any more. How hard can we expect even a pair of magic shoes to work? Are metaphors comprehensible to them, abstractions permissible, redefinitions acceptable? Are we asking too much? As our needs emerge from their redoubts and press in upon the electrified glass, will the shoes, like the Grimms' ancient flat-fish, lose patience with our demands and return us to the piss-pots whence we came?

The presence of imaginary beings in the Saleroom may be the last straw. Children from nineteenth-century Australian realist paintings are here, whining from their ornate, gilded frames about being lost in the immensity of the outback. In blue smocks and ankle socks they gaze into rain forests and deserts. A literary character, condemned to an eternity of reading the works of Dickens to an armed madman in a jungle, has sent in a written bid. I notice, on a television monitor, the frail figure of an alien creature with an illuminated fingertip. This permeation of the real world by the fictional is a symptom of the moral decay of the culture of the millennium. Heroes step down off cinema screens and marry members of the audience. Will there be no end to it? Is the state employing insufficient violence? Should there be more rigorous controls? We debate such questions often. There can be little doubt that a large majority of us opposes the free, unrestricted migration of imaginary beings into an already damaged reality. Few of us, after all, would choose to travel in the opposite direction (though there are reports of an increase in such migrations latterly). I shelve such debates for the moment. The Auction is about to begin.

It is necessary that I speak about my cousin Gail, and her habit of moaning loudly while making love. My cousin Gail—let me be frank—is the love of my life, and even now that we have parted I can't forget the pleasure I derived from her noisiness. I hasten to add that except for this volubility there was nothing abnormal about our love-making, nothing, if I may put it thus, *fictional*. Yet it satisfied me deeply, especially when she cried out at

250

the moment of penetration, 'Home, boy! Home, baby—you've come home!' One day, however, I came home to find her in the arms of a hairy escapee from a cave man movie. I moved out the same day, weeping my way down the street with my large portrait of Gail in the guise of a tornado cradled in my arms and my collection of old Pat Boone 78 r.p.m. records in a rucksack on my back. This happened many years ago. For a time after Gail dumped me I was bitter and would reveal to our social circle that she had lost her virginity at the age of fourteen in an accident involving a defective shooting-stick, but vindictiveness did not satisfy me for long. Since those days I have dedicated myself to her memory. I have made of myself a candle at her temple. I am aware that after all these years the Gail I adore is not entirely a real person. The real Gail has become confused with my re-imagining of her, of our life together in an alternative universe devoid of ape-men. The real Gail may by now be beyond our grasp, ineffable.

I saw her recently, in a long dark subterranean bar guarded by commandos bearing battlefield nuclear weapons. There were Polynesian snacks on the counter and beers from the Pacific basin on tap: Kirin, Tsingtao, Swan. At that time many television channels were devoted to the sad case of the astronaut stranded on Mars without hope of rescue, and with diminishing supplies of food and breathable air. The cameras inside his marooned spacecraft continued to send us poignant images of his slow descent into despair, his low-gravity, weight-reduced death. I watched my cousin Gail watching the screen, and when this condemned man on another planet began to sing a squawky medley of songs I was reminded of the dying computer in *2001: A Space Odyssey*, which sang 'Daisy, Daisy' as it was being unplugged; but my cousin Gail, hearing these spaced-out renditions of 'Swanee', 'Show Me the Way to go Home' and several numbers from *The Wizard of Oz*, began to weep. I first heard about the upcoming auction of the ruby slippers the very next morning, and resolved at once to buy them, whatever the cost. My plan was simple. I would offer them up to Gail in all humility. Perhaps I would even click the heels together three times; and I would win back her heart by murmuring softly: *There's no place like home.*

Salman Rushdie

Y**ou** laugh at my desperation. Hah! Go tell a drowning man not to grab for the passing straws. Or a dying astronaut not to sing. Come here and stand in my shoes. Step across this line. Put 'em up. Put 'em uuuup. I'll fight you with one hand tied behind my back. I'll fight you with my eyes closed. Scared, huh? Scared?

T**he** Grand Saleroom of the Auctioneers is the beating heart of the world. If you stand here for long enough all the wonders of the world will pass by. In the Grand Saleroom, in recent years, we have witnessed the auction of the Taj Mahal, the Statue of Liberty, the Sphinx. We have assisted at the sale of wives and the purchase of husbands. State secrets have been sold here, openly, to the highest bidder. On one very special occasion, the Auctioneers presided over the sale, to an overheated bunch of smouldering red demons, of a wide selection of human souls of all classes, qualities, ages, races and creeds. Everything is for sale, and under the firm yet essentially benevolent supervision of the Auctioneers, their security dogs and SWAT teams, we engage in a battle of wits and wallets, a war of nerves. There is a purity about our actions here, and also an aesthetically pleasing tension between the vast complexity of the life that turns up, packaged into lots, to go under the hammer, and the equally immense simplicity of our manner of dealing with it. We bid, the Auctioneers knock a lot down, we pass on. All are equal before the justice of the gavels: the pavement artist and Michelangelo, the slave girl and the queen. This is the courtroom of demand.

They are bidding for the slippers now. As the price rises, so does my gorge. Panic is clutching at me, pulling me down, drowning me. I think of Gail—sweet coz!—and fight back the fear, and bid.

O**nce** I was asked by the widower of a world-famous and much-loved pop singer to attend an auction of rock memorabilia on his behalf. He was the sole trustee of her estate, which was worth tens of millions; I treated him with respect. 'There's only one lot I want,' he said. 'Buy it at any price.' It was an article of clothing, a pair of edible rice-paper

252

panties in peppermint flavour, purchased long ago in a store on (I think this was the name) Rodeo Drive. My employer's late wife's stage act had included the public removal and consumption of several such pairs. More panties, in a variety of flavours—chocolate chip, knickerbocker glory, cassata—were hurled into the crowd. These, too, were gobbled up in the excitement, the lucky recipients being too carried away to consider the future value of what they had caught. Undergarments that had actually been owned by the lady were therefore in short supply, and presently in great demand. During that auction, bids came in across the video links with Tokyo, Los Angeles, Paris and Milan, and they were so rapid and of such size that I lost my nerve. However, when I telephoned my employer to confess my failure he was quite unperturbed, interested only in the price the lot had fetched. I mentioned a five-figure sum, and he laughed. It was the first truly joyful laugh I had heard from him since the day his wife died. 'That's all right then,' he said. 'I've got three hundred thousand of those.'

It is to the Auctioneers we go to establish the value of our pasts, of our futures, of our lives.

The price for the ruby slippers is rising ever higher. Many of the bidders would appear to be proxies, as I was on the day of the underpants, as I am so often, in so many ways. Today, however, I am bidding—perhaps literally—for myself.

There's an explosion in the street outside. We hear running feet, sirens, screams. Such things have become commonplace. We remain absorbed by a higher drama.

The cuspidors are in full employment. Witches keen, movie stars flounce off with tarnished auras. Queues of the disconsolate form at the psychiatrists' booths. There is work for the club-wielding guards, though not, as yet, for the obstetricians. Order is maintained. I am the only person in the Grand Saleroom still in the bidding. My rivals are disembodied heads on video screens, and unheard voices on special telephone links. I am doing battle with an invisible world of demons and ghosts, and the prize is my lady's hand.

At the height of an auction, when the money has become no more than a way of keeping score, there is a thing that happens which I am reluctant to admit: one becomes detached from the earth. There is a loss of gravity, a reduction in weight, a floating in the capsule of the struggle. The ultimate goal crosses a delirious frontier. Its achievement and our own survival become —yes!—fictions.

And fictions, as I have come close to suggesting before, are dangerous.

In fiction's grip, we may mortgage our homes, sell our children, to have whatever it is we crave. Alternatively, in that miasmal ocean, we may simply float away from our heart's desires, and see them anew, from a distance, so that they seem weightless, trivial. We let them go. Like men dying in a blizzard, we lie down in the snow to sleep.

So it is that my cousin Gail loses her hold over me in the crucible of the auction. So it is that I drop out of the bidding, and sleep.

When I awake I feel refreshed, and free.

Next week there is another auction. Family trees, coats of arms, royal lineages will be up for sale, and into any of these one may insert any name one chooses, one's own, or one's beloved's. Canine pedigrees will be on offer, too: Alsatian, saluki, cairn terrier.

Did I mention my love for my cousin Toto?

A GREAT AMERICAN
LITERARY TRADITION

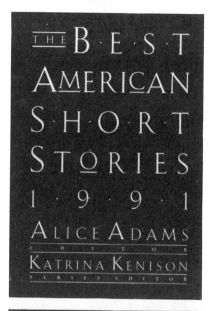

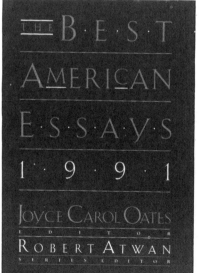

Notes on Contributors

Redmond O'Hanlon is the author of *Into the Heart of Borneo* and *In Trouble Again*. **Abraham Verghese** is Professor of Medicine at Texas Tech University in El Paso. He is working on a book about his life as a doctor during the AIDS epidemic. **Michael Dibdin**'s new book, *Cabal,* to be published in May, is the third in the Aurelio Zen series. A collection of **Mary Ellen Mark**'s photography entitled *Mary Ellen Mark: 25 Years* was published earlier this year. **Jeanette Winterson**'s story is part of a novel entitled *Written on the Body* which will be published by Jonathan Cape in the autumn. **Geoffrey Biddle** married Mary Ann Unger in 1980. Their daughter Eve was born in 1982. Among the pictures of his parents and his family in this issue are two taken by his daughter on pages 152 and 154. **Todd McEwen,** a former editor at *Granta,* is currently living in California. His second novel, *McX,* was recently published in paperback. *The Law of White Spaces,* a book of **Giorgio Pressburger**'s stories concerning illness of the mind and body, was published by Granta Books in March. **Hanif Kureishi**'s novella 'With Your Tongue Down My Throat' appeared in *Granta* 22. The Czech photographer **Antonin Kratochvil** lives in New York. A collection of his photographs of Eastern Europe, *Work in Progress*, will be published in 1993. **Anchee Min** left Red Fire Farm in 1976 when she was selected to act in propaganda films at the Shanghai Film Studios. She emigrated from China in 1984 and now lives in Chicago. 'Red Fire Farm' is her first published work. **John Conroy** is the author of *Belfast Diary: War as a Way of Life.* He also lives in Chicago, where he is working on a book about torture. **Peregrine Hodson**'s book *A Circle Round the Sun: A Foreigner in Japan* will be published in June. **Victoria Tokareva**'s stories 'Centre of Gravity' and 'Dry Run' appeared in *Granta*s 30 and 33. **Salman Rushdie**'s *Imaginary Homelands* was published in paperback by Granta Books on 14 February. It includes a new essay, 'One Thousand Days in A Balloon', written to mark the third anniversary of the Iranian fatwa. 'At the Auction of the Ruby Slippers' will be included with his appreciation of *The Wizard of Oz* in the British Film Institute's new 'Film Classics' series, to be published in May.

Correction: The cover photo for *Granta* 38 was wrongly attributed to Eve Arnold.